Edward Carter is Canon Theologia
degrees in economics and theology,
studies in Christian ethics at Oxford .... *ın ∠∪∪∪. He is a member*
of the Ethical Investment Advisory Group of the Church of England.
Edward is married to Sarah and they have two teenage sons.

Barnabas
in
Schools

Text copyright © Edward Carter & Jo Fageant 2012
The authors assert the moral right
to be identified as the authors of this work

Published by
The Bible Reading Fellowship
15 The Chambers, Vineyard
Abingdon OX14 3FE
United Kingdom
Tel: +44 (0)1865 319700
Email: enquiries@brf.org.uk
Website: www.brf.org.uk
BRF is a Registered Charity

ISBN 978 0 85746 059 2

First published 2012
10 9 8 7 6 5 4 3 2 1 0

Acknowledgments
Unless otherwise stated, scripture quotations are taken from the Good News Bible published
by The Bible Societies/HarperCollins Publishers Ltd, UK © American Bible Society 1966,
1971, 1976, 1992, and are used with permission.

Scripture quotations from the Contemporary English Version © American Bible Society 1991,
1992, 1995. Used by permission/Anglicisations © British and Foreign Bible Society 1997.

The paper used in the production of this publication was supplied by mills that source their
raw materials from sustainably managed forests. Soy-based inks were used in its printing and
the laminate film is biodegradable.

A catalogue record for this book is available from the British Library

Printed in Singapore by Craft Print International Ltd

Story Assemblies
for the School Year
Volume 2

36 assemblies with five-minute stories, teacher's notes and
RE follow-up

Edward J Carter

Ideas for classroom follow-up by Jo Fageant

Dedicated to the children of Northbourne School
in Didcot, who heard these stories when
they were first being told.

Comments from people who have used the prototype material

We've been very much enjoying this year's stories. 'The game of block-blast' is perhaps the most popular so far, a big hit with the whole age range of pupils!

In 'The pioneer's drum'... the children very quickly learned to clap the appropriate tunes.

'The chef's weighing scales' is a fantastic story, which I am thoroughly enjoying telling.

God's Storyteller is going well: the children are really enjoying 'The chef's weighing scales'.

I feel that the time invested in creating a good-quality prop is time well spent, as they engage the children so well.

Reviews of 'Story Assemblies for the School Year'

A really useful resource for primary schools, with assemblies arranged into sets of six episodes, each with a final celebration. There is enough material here for a whole school year and it includes five-minute stories, suggestions for follow-up work, ideas for music (complete with sources) and prayer. There is also a website for further information.

THE BOOKSELLER

I like the way this book is constructed, skilfully exploring the Christian faith and presenting pupils with the opportunity to reflect on spiritual and moral issues.

LESLEY BEADLE, RE TODAY

The stories are interesting and often finish on a cliffhanger, making the children want to know what happens next. The assembly continues relating the story to the Bible story… There is a visual prompt for each theme, which is great for all ages. The language of the stories is familiar and the stories build on each other well. It's an easy book to just pick up and take to the assembly and read out. It's ideal for a class teacher taking assemblies and suitable for the non-specialist RE teacher.

RACHEL DAVEY, THE ASSOCIATION OF CHRISTIAN TEACHERS

Preface

Children love stories, and I've really enjoyed telling the stories in this book when leading assemblies. I wanted to keep my assemblies broadly Christian by telling the big story of God's love for the world, and I've tried to make it fun by helping the children imagine themselves as part of the story as well. It encourages them to think about their own values and behaviour, not by learning the right answers to give but by making a leap of imagination and identifying themselves with the characters in the stories.

My stories are in the tradition of great Christian storytellers such as C.S. Lewis and his Narnia Chronicles, but designed for school assemblies. Jesus himself taught using parables and, in a similar way, the stories in this book are essentially parables about God and the events in the Bible. If you use them all, they take you through the whole school year.

The first collection of my stories was published under the title *Story Assemblies for the School Year* (BRF/Barnabas, 2010), and was very well received. I'm delighted to be sharing this next set of stories with you as well.

Edward Carter

Contents

Section Three: The disciples of Jesus 79

Values: Friendship and exploration

Story: The pioneer's drum

Section Four: The judgment parables 111

Values: Pride and forgiveness

Story: The chef's weighing scales

*

Introduction

There are many ways you could use the material in this book, but it has been designed so that the main story episodes are told once a week. At the end of each set of six episodes there is a final celebration, which connects to a seasonal theme such as Christmas or Easter.

Before the first assembly you will need to:

- Choose someone (or several people to take it in turns) to be the storyteller.
- Make the storyteller's prop for the story in question, using the instructions.
- Quickly run through the first story episode so that it is familiar.

Extra things that you could do to increase the impact of the stories include:

- Make a badge for the storyteller to wear (the wording on the badge could be 'God's Storyteller').
- Make a display board on which children's work, connected to the stories, can be displayed.
- Choose suitable music to be played before and after the assembly.
- Choose a song to sing at the assembly that links to the story episode.
- Use your classroom-based follow-up time to connect to the stories.
- Keep the teaching staff informed about the stories and advise them about good curriculum links.

Suggestions are given throughout the book on how these ideas can best be put into practice.

There are two ways of telling the stories. You can either read them in full from this book, as you would from any book you are using for a story, or you can tell the story without a script, using notes as prompts. A storyteller's notes card for each episode is available to download from the website www.barnabasinschools.org.uk/extra-resources/. You can also download the key Bible verse card for each story from this website. The storyteller's prop helps to illustrate the story and acts as a good prompt in itself.

Although the material in this book has been designed for use in school assemblies, it can also be used as the basis for an RE course focused on Christianity.

Year Outline

Story Assemblies for the School Year Volume 2 includes material for one school year. The year is divided into six sections, corresponding to the six blocks of teaching time.

Section One: The exodus
Values: Freedom and courage
Story: Grandad's cereal box
Key Bible verse: 'God said, "I have seen the cruel suffering of my people in Egypt. I have heard their groans, and I have come down to set them free"' (Acts 7:34).
Concluding celebration: Harvest

Section Two: The promised land
Values: Cooperation and perseverance
Story: The game of block-blast
Key Bible verses: 'Obey all the laws that I have given you today. Then you will be able to cross the river and occupy the land that you are about to enter' (Deuteronomy 11:8–9).
Concluding celebration: Christmas

Section Three: The disciples of Jesus
Values: Friendship and exploration
Story: The pioneer's drum
Key Bible verse: 'Jesus said, "Whoever wants to serve me must follow me"' (John 12:26).
Concluding celebration: Lent

Section Four: The judgment parables
Values: Pride and forgiveness
Story: The chef's weighing scales
Key Bible verses: 'God has weighed you on his balance scales, and you fall short of what it takes' (Daniel 5:27, CEV); 'Christ himself carried our sins in his body to the cross, so that we might die to sin and live for righteousness. It is by his wounds that you have been healed' (1 Peter 2:24); 'Those who win the victory will be clothed like this in white, and I will not remove their names from the book of the living' (Revelation 3:5).
Concluding celebration: Holy Week or Easter

Section Five: The first Christians
Values: Happiness and unity
Story: Pavlov's power-suit
Key Bible verse: 'All of you are Christ's body, and each one is a part of it' (1 Corinthians 12:27).
Concluding celebration: Pentecost

Section Six: Paul's letters
Values: Loyalty and self-discovery
Story: Hyperlink Harita
Key Bible verse: 'We who have this spiritual treasure are like common clay pots, in order to show that the supreme power belongs to God, not to us' (2 Corinthians 4:7).
Concluding celebration: Leavers' farewell

*

The exodus

Key Bible verse

God said, 'I have seen the cruel suffering of my people in Egypt.
I have heard their groans, and I have come down
to set them free.'

ACTS 7:34

Values

Freedom and courage

This section is designed to run from the start of the school year in September through to the October break. The theme is 'The exodus' and, in the big story of God's love for the world, we are remembering the time when he set his chosen people free from slavery in Egypt. When we imagine ourselves within this part of the story, we discover what it feels like to be set free from things that worry us or prevent us from being ourselves. We also realise that sometimes we have to show courage.

'Grandad's cereal box' is a story told in six parts plus a final harvest time episode, which illustrates the biblical account of the escape of Moses and the Israelites from slavery under Pharaoh in Egypt. It is found mainly in the book of Exodus.

- **Week One:** Genesis 41:53–57; 45:7–8
- **Week Two:** Exodus 1:8–14
- **Week Three:** Exodus 8:1–6, 16–17, 20–24; 10:12–15
- **Week Four:** Exodus 12:1–11; 14:19–29
- **Week Five:** Exodus 16:2–18
- **Week Six:** Exodus 19:16–20; 20:1–17

The storyteller's prop consists of a large cereal box labelled 'Doctor Dan's Extremely Crumbly & Crunchy Cereal Cubes' and a smaller box containing dried pasta, which makes a rattling noise. The smaller box should fit tightly inside the main cereal box.

Suggested music

Suggestions for pre-recorded music that could be used at the start and end of assemblies include:

- 'Go down, Moses' (*Famous Spirituals*, Philips B0000060BG)
- Music from *Joseph and the Amazing Technicolor Dreamcoat* (Polydor B000001DUI)

Suggestions for songs that could be sung at assemblies include:

- Father, I place into your hands
- Give me joy in my heart
- How did Moses cross the Red Sea?
- I, the Lord of sea and sky
- Thank you, Lord, for this new day
- We are marching in the light of God

*

Grandad's cereal box: Week One

Bible link

This week's Bible passage link is Genesis 41:53–57 and 45:7–8, which recounts the famine that struck when Joseph was in Egypt and the way in which God used Joseph to provide food for his chosen people.

Key theme

This week's key theme is 'being alone and being lonely'. Consider the positive and negative aspects of being alone. Being lonely can be like imprisonment in oneself. The story talks about feelings of imprisonment. Explore different meanings of this word and different ways of being imprisoned. What do they all have in common?

Episode One

(Prepare the cereal box so that it rattles when shaken.)

I wonder if any of you went away from home this summer holiday. Maybe you even went somewhere new and strange, where you'd never been before. Today I want to start telling you a story about two children who went to stay with their grandad one summer. It's a very special story, because it also tells us about God and about something very important that happened in the Bible.

Once upon a time, two children called Pip and Polly, who lived in a big city, went to stay with their old grandad, who lived by the sea. One day it was so wet that they couldn't go out at all. Grandad always needed his afternoon rest, so, while he was asleep, Pip and Polly decided to explore the house. When they got to the kitchen, they opened every cupboard and found all sorts of knives and forks and plates and saucepans. But the best cupboard was the larder, where Grandad kept his food. Right at the back, covered in dust, was a very old cereal box. *(Show the cereal box.)*

Pip and Polly read the name of the cereal: 'Doctor Dan's Extremely Crumbly & Crunchy Cereal Cubes'. The box seemed so old, they wondered if there was anything left inside and if it was still safe to eat. So they gave the box a shake. *(Shake the box to make a rattling noise.)* Just then, they heard Grandad coming downstairs. They didn't have time to put everything back, but Grandad wasn't cross when he saw them with the cereal box. 'There's quite a story that goes with this,' he said. 'Would you like to hear it?' Pip and Polly nodded their heads excitedly, so Grandad began.

'Many years ago, I was on a ship on a faraway ocean. The ship got caught in a storm and it hit some rocks. Everyone else managed to escape on a lifeboat, but I was knocked out and nobody remembered to rescue me. When I woke up again, I was all alone on the wreck, but I could see an island, so I swam to it. It was horrible being completely alone. It felt like a prison. I can remember what I said: "I don't like it here. When will I ever be free?"

'I didn't have anything to eat but, luckily, on the beach there was a big case of food that had washed up from the wreck. When I looked inside, it had loads of delicious things, so I tucked in. The food in the case lasted seven whole weeks, but no one came to rescue me. In the end there was no food left, and then I started to get really hungry. I can remember what I said: "I don't like it here. When will I ever be free?"

'Luckily, I had one last look inside the case of food. Hidden at the bottom was that cereal box, full of Doctor Dan's Extremely Crumbly & Crunchy Cereal Cubes. So I gave the box a shake (*shake the box*) and poured out some cereal. There wasn't anything else at all to eat, so I was very lucky to have that box. The amazing thing was, it kept on pouring out cereal cubes day after day. In fact, it lasted for another seven whole weeks.

'I can remember what I said to myself then: "It's quite nice on this island. Maybe I'll be happy to stay here for ever!" But that's not the whole of the story. That's just when things started to go badly wrong...'

Pip and Polly were listening eagerly, but I haven't got time to tell any more of the story about Grandad and his mysterious cereal box today. Next time I'll tell you some more, and maybe we'll discover what went wrong. But it's a very special story, because it reminds us about some people in the Bible and how God helped them.

There was a man called Jacob, but God gave him another name: 'Israel'. His children and their families were called the Israelites, and God knew he had to take care of them. One of Jacob's sons was called Joseph. Joseph had a coat of many colours, but he lost his coat and ended up in the land of Egypt. God helped him so much that when seven years of famine came, he could help the other Israelites survive.

Grandad reminds us of the Israelites. He was shipwrecked on a strange island, just as the Israelites had to go to Egypt, a strange land. When Grandad found the mysterious cereal box that kept him alive, it was just like the food that the Israelites got from Joseph. But although the cereal cubes kept Grandad alive, he knew that the island wasn't really a nice place to be. The Israelites were the same. They found food in Egypt but they knew it wasn't really their home. They knew they weren't really free.

If you'd been Grandad, stuck on the island, I wonder how you'd have felt. Would you have enjoyed Doctor Dan's Extremely Crumbly & Crunchy Cereal Cubes? (*Shake the box.*) Would you have wanted to stay on the island or escape from it? And if you'd been one of the Israelites, stuck in Egypt, I wonder how you'd have felt. Would you have been happy to stay or would you have asked God to help you escape? I wonder.

Possible concluding prayer

Lord God, you help people when they're in danger, and you promise to set your people free. When the Israelites were starving, you kept them safe by feeding them in Egypt. Help us to be filled with courage when things aren't going well, and help us to trust you each and every day. Amen

Grandad's cereal box: Week Two

Bible link

This week's Bible passage link is Exodus 1:8–14, which recounts the way in which the Egyptian rulers persecuted the Israelites while they lived in Egypt.

Key theme

This week's key theme is 'hunger'. Consider the importance of good and varied food for a healthy lifestyle, and aspects of a healthy diet.

Episode Two

(Prepare the cereal box so that it rattles when shaken.)

Do you remember the story we began hearing last week? Who was stuck on an island? What did Grandad use to help him survive when he was hungry? *(Produce the cereal box and rattle it.)*

Do you remember how this story about Grandad's cereal box reminds us of the Israelites in Egypt and how God gave them food when they were starving?

Pip and Polly were still listening to Grandad and he carried on telling his story.

'I'd been on the island for 14 weeks, but I wanted to be free again because it felt like a prison. The only food left was the box of Doctor Dan's Extremely Crumbly & Crunchy Cereal Cubes (*shake the box*), which always gave me enough to eat. But then things started going badly wrong.

'There were animals on the island—mice and snakes and a dog and lizards, and even some small monkeys—and they were all getting hungry too. They knew that the cereal box was the easiest way of getting food. Each morning they watched me as I shook the box (*shake the box*) and ate some more cereal cubes.

'One day, when I was having a wash in the sea, I noticed one of the monkeys trying to pick up the box of Doctor Dan's Extremely Crumbly & Crunchy Cereal Cubes. The monkey was quite small, so it wasn't easy for him to carry it, but I was horrified! The cereal box held my only supply of food, so I ran back up the beach, shouting at the monkey at the top of my voice. Luckily I got the cereal box back, but I could see it wouldn't be long before another animal tried to steal it.

'My first idea was to hide the cereal box up a tree, so I found a palm tree and I hid the box up in the leaves where no one could see it. But the monkeys noticed it, and they climbed up to try and grab it. I scared them away just in time, but I could see I needed a better idea.

'Next I tried using one of the wooden cases lying on the beach, washed up from the wreck. I put the cereal box carefully inside the case and fixed the lid on tight. But I noticed some mice nibbling away at the wood. Their teeth were very sharp and before long they'd made a hole. I had to frighten them away, but the cereal box wasn't safe in the wooden case any more.

'Then I had a brilliant idea. I put the cereal box on a big wooden plank and I let the plank float out to sea, with a rope tied to it so that I could pull it back in. To start with, everything was fine, but then the dog saw the plank and swam out to try to get it. I only just managed to pull it back in time!

'I was growing desperate by then. Where would the box of Doctor Dan's Extremely Crumbly & Crunchy Cereal Cubes be safe? Then suddenly I knew the answer. I dug a big hole in the ground, put the cereal box in, and covered it over with earth and sand (hide the box). None of the animals could possibly get it now.

'At the next meal-time, with no cereal box, there was nothing for me to eat. Gradually I got hungrier and hungrier, and I got weaker and weaker. I can remember what I said: "I don't like it here. When will I ever be free?" So then I knew there was only one thing I could do...'

Pip and Polly were still listening eagerly, but I haven't got time to tell any more of the story about Grandad and his mysterious cereal box today. Next time I'll tell you some more and we'll discover what Grandad did. But it's a very special story, because it reminds us about the Israelites and how God helped them.

The Israelites were living in Egypt and God had helped them in the past, when Joseph was Pharaoh's friend. But now a new Pharaoh was ruler and he hated the Israelites. He wanted to finish them off once and for all, so he did horrible things to them.

Grandad, who was shipwrecked on the strange island, reminds us of the Israelites, who were in Egypt, a strange land. Although the Israelites had been all right in the past, just like Grandad getting food from the cereal box, the time came when they didn't have enough food and their enemies oppressed them. It was just like Grandad, who was pestered by the animals on the island so much that he had to bury the cereal box. Then he began to get hungrier and hungrier. Just as Grandad wanted to escape, to be free again, so the Israelites also wanted to be free, to escape from Egypt.

If you'd been Grandad, stuck on the island, I wonder how you'd have felt. Would you have buried the box like he did, when all the animals pestered him? And if you'd been one of the Israelites, stuck in Egypt, I wonder how you'd have felt when Pharaoh was your enemy. Would you have asked God to help you break free? I wonder.

Possible concluding prayer

Lord God, you help people when they're in danger and you promise to set your people free. When the Israelites were persecuted in Egypt, you never forgot them. Help us to be filled with courage when things aren't going well, and help us to trust you each and every day. Amen

Grandad's cereal box: Week Three

Bible link

This week's Bible passage link is Exodus 8:1–6, 16–17 and 20–24, and 10:12–15, which recounts the plagues that were sent against the land of Egypt when Pharaoh refused to let the Israelites go.

Key theme

This week's key theme is 'perseverance'. Sometimes we have to persevere at something even when times are hard, things go wrong and we want to give up. Think about how it feels to stick something out and get through, as well as how it feels to give up and not succeed.

Episode Three

(Prepare the cereal box so that it does not rattle when shaken. Keep it hidden to start with.)

Do you remember our story from last time? What was the name of the cereal that Grandad had found? Why was he so hungry again?

Do you remember how this story about Grandad's cereal box reminds us of the Israelites in Egypt, and how Pharaoh was horrible to them and treated them like slaves?

Pip and Polly were still listening to Grandad and he carried on telling his story.

'I was getting hungrier and hungrier and I wanted to escape from the island more and more each day. I wanted to be free! But I knew I needed food from the cereal box. I needed Doctor Dan's Extremely Crumbly & Crunchy Cereal Cubes more than anything else in the world. So I decided to dig the box up again, even though the animals were all watching me still.

'In the end, I found the place where the box was buried. I was so weak, it took me ages to dig down into the ground, but finally I reached the cereal box. *(Carefully produce the cereal box and put it on the floor.)* I was so pleased to have it in my hands again, even though it was very damp. I decided to shake it, to make sure everything was all right *(shake the box vigorously)*, but it didn't make any noise at all.

'I couldn't understand why the box didn't rattle properly, so I carefully opened the lid and looked inside. What I saw made my insides squirm. There were horrible little insects crawling everywhere inside the box, and even some tiny frogs that must have burrowed down underground. The special cereal cubes were all spoilt! No wonder they didn't rattle nicely any more. All the food was ruined and even the animals didn't seem to be interested.

'Then I knew I would have to try to escape from the island. I was desperate to be free. So I started building a raft out of bits of wood on the beach. It was very difficult because the pieces of wood were all different shapes and sizes, and I had to use vines from the jungle to tie them together. I was feeling very weak and, even worse, as soon as I'd tied one bit of the raft properly, the monkeys would run up and untie the knot! Making a raft was impossible.

'Luckily, I'd noticed that one of the jungle plants had massive leaves, perfect for making a little sailing boat. It took ages to finish, but in the end I managed to float the boat on the sea and the wind carried it out nicely. I was about to start celebrating my escape when the dog came swimming along and barged straight into the boat. It was so flimsy that the water came rushing in, and I had to swim quickly back to the beach.

'I thought I'd never escape from the island, especially with all the animals ruining everything I tried. After a bit, though, I decided to try making a big glider, using bamboo poles and more of the big leaves, all tied together with the vines. I worked on the glider for days and finally it was ready. I climbed in and started flapping the wings, but the glider didn't take off. I couldn't understand why it wasn't working, but suddenly I noticed lots of little holes in the wings. The mice had nibbled through them.

'After that, I was so exhausted, I just fell down on the sand, ready to cry. I was desperate to escape from the island, but every time something had gone wrong. The animals hadn't let me go. As I looked around, I knew there was only one thing left I could do...'

Pip and Polly were still listening eagerly, but I haven't got time to tell any more of the story about Grandad and his mysterious cereal box today. Next time I'll tell you some more and we'll discover what Grandad did. But it's a very special story, because it reminds us about the Israelites and how God helped them.

The Israelites were living in Egypt, but it was a horrible place. They were Pharaoh's slaves and he wouldn't let them go. So God sent plagues of insects and frogs and other nasty things to frighten Pharaoh and the Egyptians. But whenever the Israelites were about to escape, Pharaoh stopped them at the last minute.

Grandad, who was shipwrecked on the strange island, reminds us of the Israelites, who were in Egypt, a strange land. The Israelites didn't have enough food because Pharaoh was being horrible to them and because of all the plagues, just as Grandad was hungry because his cereal box had become useless. And just as Grandad tried to escape from the island to be free again, so the Israelites also tried to escape from Egypt, but Pharaoh stopped them each time.

If you'd been Grandad, stuck on the island, I wonder how you'd have felt when the cereal box was ruined. How would you have tried to escape? I bet the animals would have stopped you as well. And if you'd been one of the Israelites in Egypt, how would you have felt when Pharaoh persecuted you and wouldn't let you go free? I wonder if you'd have asked God for help. I wonder.

Possible concluding prayer

Lord God, you help people when they're in danger and you promise to set your people free. When the Israelites were slaves in Egypt, you heard their prayers. Help us to be filled with courage when things aren't going well, and help us to trust you each and every day. Amen

*

Grandad's cereal box: Week Four

Bible link

This week's Bible passage link is Exodus 12:1–11 and 14:19–29, which recounts the Passover meal that the Israelites ate and their escape from Pharaoh's army through the Red Sea.

Key theme

This week's key theme is 'facing danger'. Consider different reactions to being in situations of danger. How do people cope with dangerous situations? How do people find inner strength and resolve? What situations of danger might a person of your age find themselves in? How can you best avoid these situations?

Episode Four

(Prepare the cereal box so that it does rattle again when shaken. At the start, it should be placed in view.)

Do you remember our story from last time? Who was stuck on an island? What had happened to the cereal box? And why couldn't Grandad manage to escape?

Do you remember how this story about Grandad's cereal box reminds us of the Israelites in Egypt and how Pharaoh wouldn't let them go, even though God sent plagues of insects and frogs and other nasty things?

Pip and Polly were still listening to Grandad. His voice was all croaky.

'By now I was so weak, I could hardly even crawl. But as I lay on the beach, I noticed the shipwreck out in the bay. The tall mast was sticking high up in the air, the perfect place from which to signal for help. So I decided to try to swim out through the water to the wreck. I managed to crawl down the beach into the sea but, just when I was out of my depth, those annoying animals—the monkeys, the dog and the mice—came and blocked my way, so I had to splash back to the island. By now I was so weak, I knew I needed food before I could escape.

'So I began searching the island. I could see some bananas up a tree, but they were way out of reach. I even found some nuts, but the shells were too strong for me to break open. I couldn't find anything to eat, and that evening I crawled back to the beach, still with an empty tummy. The only thing there was the box of Doctor Dan's Extremely Crumbly & Crunchy Cereal Cubes. I knew that the cereal cubes were all spoilt, but by then I was desperate. I started talking to the box: "Please give me some food! Please! Just one bowlful!" I thought it was hopeless, but, as I gave the box a shake (*shake the box so that it rattles noisily*), I couldn't believe my ears! It made a lovely rattling noise and I poured out the cereal cubes, all fresh and delicious. They made a lovely meal.

'Suddenly I was feeling strong and brave again. I took the box and walked quickly down to the sea again, plunged into the water and started swimming out towards the shipwreck, towards freedom. I could swim strongly again now, but, as the wreck drew near, my heart almost stopped beating. Up ahead, blocking my way, were about 20 crocodiles, flashing their teeth at me and twisting about in the water!

'I was about to turn back when I noticed that the sky had

gone dark. A strong wind had started blowing and the water was making bigger and bigger waves. A storm was on its way. The island was too far behind me, so I had to carry on to the wreck, even though the crocodiles were coming. They were snapping their jaws fiercely, but the cereal cubes made me so courageous that I kept going. By now the waves were as tall as houses. The crocodiles were trying to swim towards me, but the water was pushing them back. Even their powerful tails couldn't stop them being smashed on to the rocks one by one. The waves had saved me and, as I reached the wreck, I scrambled up the side, shouting for joy. But then I saw a very sad sight...'

Pip and Polly were still listening eagerly, but I haven't got time for any more of the story about Grandad and his mysterious cereal box today. Next time I'll tell you some more and we'll discover what Grandad saw. But it's a very special story, because it reminds us about the Israelites and how God helped them.

The Israelites were living in Egypt and they were desperate to escape. They prayed to God for help and God told Moses that they should all have a special meal, the 'Passover' meal. God would strike down the Egyptians but he would 'pass over' the Israelites so that they could escape. They escaped by crossing the Red Sea, because God pushed the waves back. Pharaoh couldn't stop them. Moses and the Israelites were full of courage. They actually managed to escape and to be free from the Egyptians.

Grandad, who was shipwrecked on the island, reminds us of the Israelites, who were stuck in Egypt. Pharaoh was trying to stop the Israelites escaping but, in the end, they prayed to God and they had that special meal, the Passover, just as the cereal box gave Grandad a special bowlful just when he needed it. After that, Grandad, using all his courage, managed to swim off the island. He escaped from the island, just as Moses and the Israelites escaped from Egypt. The crocodiles couldn't stop Grandad, and Pharaoh's chariots couldn't stop the Israelites.

If you'd been Grandad, stuck on the island, I wonder how you'd have felt when the cereal box rattled again. Would you have been brave enough to swim towards the crocodiles? And if you'd been with the Israelites in Egypt, I wonder how you'd have felt, eating that Passover meal? Would you have been brave enough to go with Moses across the Red Sea, with Pharaoh's chariots chasing you? I wonder what it felt like, escaping to freedom. I wonder.

Possible concluding prayer

Lord God, you help people when they're in danger and you promise to set your people free. When the Israelites were slaves in Egypt, you brought them safely through the Red Sea and helped them escape from Pharaoh's chariots. Help us to be filled with courage when things aren't going well, and help us to trust you each and every day. Amen

*

Grandad's cereal box: Week Five

Bible link

This week's Bible passage link is Exodus 16:2–18, which recounts the way in which the Israelites grumbled in the wilderness because they were hungry, and how God sent them food.

Key theme

This week's key theme is 'loss and disappointment'. Everyone loses things or people that are important to them and has to deal with feelings of loss. Talk about how it feels to lose something important. What are the most important things to you, that you would least like to lose? Grandad survived for a long time with almost nothing. What does that say about what is really important in life?

Episode Five

(Prepare the cereal box so that it rattles when shaken.)

Do you remember our story from last time? How did Grandad manage to escape from the island?

Do you remember how this story about Grandad's cereal box reminds us of the Israelites in Egypt and how they escaped from Pharaoh?

Pip and Polly were still listening to Grandad as he carried on telling his story.

'I'd made it to the shipwreck, but when I pulled myself on

to the deck, I was horrified. The ship had a great big crack all the way across. The metal bits were rusty and breaking apart, and the glass in all the windows was broken. Just then, a big wave hit the ship and a piece of wood dropped down from the mast. I only just managed to jump out of the way as it crashed to the deck.

'I was terrified, but I remembered how courageous I'd felt when I was swimming across to the ship to escape from the island, so I tried to be brave again. I wanted to find my cabin, which was down some steps. As I climbed down, I could see a very sad sight. The door of my cabin had disappeared.

'I peered through the doorway, but the whole cabin had disappeared down into the sea as well. All my clothes, my books, the photographs of my family, my little leather bag of money—it had all gone! I was so upset, I almost started to cry, but then I got angry. I started shouting: "Why did I even bother to swim over from the island? I'd have been better staying there! It's that stupid cereal box's fault! Stupid box!" But the box just stood there without making a sound. I was so tired, I collapsed on the deck of the ship, but I knew I still wanted to be free from this place. I knew I wanted to get home.

'Then I remembered the tall mast in the middle of the ship and my plan to climb to the top and shoot a bright flare into the sky, so that someone would come and rescue me. I was so weak, I needed some energy before I could begin looking. I looked at the cereal box again and read the words: "Doctor Dan's Extremely Crumbly & Crunchy Cereal Cubes". I remembered how delicious those cereal cubes were, but I felt bad because I'd shouted, "Stupid box" at it. I was worried it wouldn't give me any food because of what I'd said.

'Slowly I picked up the box and then I gave it a shake *(shake the box so that it rattles)*, and it rattled nicely. I poured out a good helping of cereal cubes and had a feast. They tasted like the best food I'd ever had, and there was just the right amount. It made me feel much stronger and I started to search the ship for some flares. To start with, I couldn't think where to look. I tried looking in the engine room and in the captain's cabin, but I couldn't find any flares at all. Then suddenly I remembered about the lifeboat. Inside it was a big box full of special things to help you survive. There were lifejackets and bottles of water and even blankets. Right at the bottom was one flare, so I put it in one of my pockets and walked to the bottom of the mast. Then I started to climb up...'

Pip and Polly were still listening eagerly, but I haven't got time for any more of the story about Grandad and his mysterious cereal box today. Next time I'll tell you some more and we'll discover if Grandad managed to climb up the mast. But it's a very special story, because it reminds us about the Israelites and how God helped them.

The Israelites had lived in Egypt for ages and they wanted to be free, but, once they'd crossed the Red Sea, they found themselves in a wilderness, a horrible place. So they started grumbling to Moses about how they wished they'd never left Egypt after all. They thought God had let them down, but then God sent them food in the wilderness, called 'manna'. So the Israelites felt courageous again and kept going.

Grandad, who'd bravely escaped from the island, reminds us of the Israelites who escaped from Egypt to freedom. The Israelites found that after they'd escaped, the wilderness was a horrible place, just as Grandad found that the ship was a horrible place, all rusty and dangerous. Grandad shouted, 'Stupid box!' just like the Israelites, who got angry with Moses and with God. But God sent the Israelites manna in the wilderness, just like the fantastic meal of cereal cubes that Grandad had from the box. It gave him the courage to carry on with his plan to find freedom. The Israelites were the same. They wanted to be free.

If you'd been Grandad on the shipwreck, I wonder how you'd have felt when you saw your cabin had disappeared, along with all your special things. Would you have got angry with the cereal box? And if you'd been with the Israelites as they travelled through the wilderness, would you have been angry with Moses and with God? I wonder how you would have felt when God sent manna to feed you. I wonder.

Possible concluding prayer

Lord God, you help people when they're in danger and you promise to set your people free. When the Israelites grumbled in the wilderness, you heard them and sent them food from heaven. Help us to be filled with courage when things aren't going well, and help us to trust you each and every day. Amen

*

Grandad's cereal box: Week Six

Bible link

This week's Bible passage link is Exodus 19:16–20 and 20:1–17, which recounts how Moses went up Mount Sinai and was given the Ten Commandments from God.

Key theme

This week's key theme is 'appreciation'. How do we show appreciation? Do we do it enough? How could we do better? What difference does it make to show appropriate appreciation for things and people?

Episode Six

(Prepare the cereal box so it rattles when shaken.)

Do you remember our story from last week? Who was stuck on an island? Where did Grandad manage to swim to? Can you remember his plan to signal for help?

Do you remember how this story about Grandad's cereal box reminds us of the Israelites in Egypt and how they managed to escape into the wilderness?

Pip and Polly were still listening to Grandad and he carried on telling his story.

'The mast was very tall, but I knew I had to climb all the way to the top. Before I started, I felt in my pocket to make sure the flare was still safely there. I was really hoping the flare was going to save me, because I wanted to be free from that place for ever. Luckily, the meal I'd had from the cereal box made me strong again, so I was feeling courageous.

'I started climbing and soon I was halfway up, but then a big flock of seagulls came swooping down. The birds started trying to peck me with their big yellow beaks, and their narrow eyes glinted in the sunshine. They seemed to be crying, 'Go back! Go back!' but I held on tight. I even shooed them away using my arms and legs, because the cereal cubes had made me so brave.

'Once the seagulls had gone, I kept on climbing. Soon the crow's nest, right at the top of the mast, was just above me. I was worried that the flare would fall, but somehow I climbed on to the tiny platform at the top of the mast, with sweat running down my face.

'Once I'd got my breath back, I reached to my pocket for the flare and pulled it out. It had a piece of special string coming down from it, which you had to light. Carefully I struck a match and held it near the string, but the wind blew it out. I tried another match, and another. Each time, the wind stopped it burning. Then I remembered the cereal box. I stood it upright and sheltered the flare and the match behind it.

'At last the string caught light! It fizzed and made sparks as the flame raced up towards the flare. Then suddenly there was smoke everywhere and a great noisy roar, and flames shot high into the sky. I looked up in amazement as the flare soared above me. Anyone 50 miles away would have seen it. I searched in every direction, as far as the eye could see, but I knew it would take a day or more for anyone to arrive. All I could do was sit down and wait.

'As I sat there at the top of the mast in the warm sunshine, I looked at the box of Doctor Dan's Extremely Crumbly & Crunchy Cereal Cubes. Without that box, I wouldn't have been able to light the flare. I picked it up and gave it a shake (*shake the box so that it rattles*) and I remembered how the box had helped me every time I was stuck. 'Thank you, box!' I said. 'You've given me just what I needed to keep me going. I'll never forget you.' Then, just as I was putting the cereal box down again, I heard a noise in the distance...'

Pip and Polly were still listening eagerly, but I haven't got time for any more of Grandad's story today. It's almost finished now, so next time we'll hear the very last bit. But it's a very special story, because it reminds us about Moses and the Israelites and how God helped them.

When the Israelites travelled through the wilderness, they came to a mountain called Mount Sinai. The people waited at the bottom of the mountain, but Moses went up to the top, where there was fire and smoke, and there he was very close to God. Moses heard God speaking to him and God explained to him exactly how the people should live their lives. God gave Moses all the commandments that the Israelites needed, so that they could really be God's people. Moses wrote those commandments down, so that no one would ever forget them.

Grandad reminds us of Moses and the Israelites, who escaped from Egypt to freedom. Just as Grandad bravely climbed up the mast, so Moses bravely went up Mount Sinai. There was fire and smoke at the top of that mountain, where Moses met God, and there was fire and smoke when Grandad let the flare off at the top of the mast. Grandad knew he couldn't have done it without his cereal box, so he promised he'd never forget how the box had helped him. And Moses knew that the Israelites must never forget God's commandments if they wanted to be free.

If you'd been Grandad, climbing up that mast, I wonder how you'd have felt. It must have been great seeing all the smoke and flames as the flare shot into the sky. Would you have thanked the cereal box, like he did? And if you'd been Moses, would you have been brave enough to go up the mountain in the smoke and flames? How would you have felt when God actually spoke to you and gave you his commandments? I wonder if you'd have tried to keep them. I wonder.

Possible concluding prayer

Lord God, you help people when they're in danger and you promise to set your people free. When Moses went up the mountain, you met him in the smoke and fire and gave him just what the Israelites needed. Help us to be filled with courage when things aren't going well, and help us to trust you each and every day. Amen

*

Grandad's cereal box:
Concluding celebration

The story of Grandad's cereal box ends very successfully with a harvest thanksgiving, with suitable songs, poems, readings and prayers. You could also organise a collection of food for a local charity or sheltered housing complex. The concluding episode of the story connects to the harvest theme.

Key theme

This week's key theme is 'harvest'. Consider all the things we have that make our lives good.

Concluding episode

(Prepare the box so that it does not rattle when shaken. If possible, hide it somewhere in a display of food that has been collected for harvest. Ask the children what their favourite foods are and search for them in the display, before finally finding the cereal box.)

Do you remember the story about Grandad's cereal box? Where was Grandad trying to escape from? How did the cereal box help him?

Do you remember how this story tells us about Moses and the Israelites and how they escaped from Egypt with God's help?

Pip and Polly sat on the edge of their seats, waiting for Grandad to finish the story.

'As I sat at the top of the mast on the shipwreck, I looked at the box of Doctor Dan's Extremely Crumbly & Crunchy Cereal Cubes and I remembered all the ways it had helped me. I remembered when I first got stranded on the island and how the cereal box gave me food to survive. I remembered when I had to bury the box and how the cereal cubes got spoilt. I remembered the time when I pleaded with the box and how it fed me again so that I was strong enough to swim past the crocodiles. I remembered when I shouted at the box and said it was stupid, but it still gave me food. Then the cereal box even helped me fire the flare into the sky. "Doctor Dan's Extremely Crumbly & Crunchy Cereal Cubes are amazing," I said to myself.

'Just then I heard a strange buzzing noise, a bit like a bee. I looked around but I couldn't see any insects. The buzzing was getting louder and louder, more like a noisy motorbike, and suddenly I noticed a speck high up in the air, moving in a straight line. As I watched, I could see it getting bigger. It had wings. It was an aeroplane! I jumped up and waved my hands in the air. I so wanted to be free from the island and from the wreck. Gradually the plane circled closer. I kept waving my hands and then I scrambled quickly down the mast, shouting all the time. I could see that it was a sea-plane and, before long, it had landed right next to the wreck, on the water, which is what sea-planes can do.

'The door of the plane opened and a man dressed in a uniform stepped across on to the wreck. "We saw your flare," he said. "How did you survive for so long? You must have been here for weeks." I tried to think what to say. How could I explain? Then I had an idea. I reached down and picked up the box of

41

Doctor Dan's Extremely Crumbly & Crunchy Cereal Cubes. "It was this box that saved me," I replied. "It gave me strength and help whenever I needed it." The man looked very surprised. He couldn't understand how a box of cereal cubes could possibly have done all that. So I started explaining everything that had happened.

'I explained about when I first got stranded on the island, and how the cereal box gave me food to survive. I explained about when I had to bury the box and how the cereal cubes got spoilt. I explained about the time when I pleaded with the box and how it fed me again so that I was strong enough to swim past the crocodiles. I explained about when I shouted at the box and said it was stupid, but it still gave me food. I explained about how the cereal box had even helped me fire the flare into the sky. The man looked amazed, as though he could hardly believe it.

'I picked up the cereal box. "Listen!" I said, and I shook the box (shake the box vigorously), but it didn't make any noise at all. A tear came into my eye. I couldn't believe the box was empty, but then the man started saying something. "You don't need the cereal cubes any more now," he said. "All you need to do is to get into my plane and we can fly away. You'll be free for ever!"'

That's just what Grandad did, but he took the box of Doctor Dan's Extremely Crumbly & Crunchy Cereal Cubes with him and he never forgot how helpful those cubes had been.

That's the end of my story—a very special story. It reminds us of how God helped Moses and the Israelites escape from Egypt, by sending them food and helping them in lots of ways. It reminds us of how God helps us, too, by making sure we have enough food. That's what we thank God for at harvest time—everything he provides us with, including our favourite cereal. And the best way we can say 'thank you' to God is to share what we have, so that everyone can have enough.

We don't just need food to live, though. In the end, Grandad's cereal box didn't rattle any more (*shake the box*), but he still escaped. It's the same for us. God makes sure we have other help as well as our food, so that in our hearts we become more and more like the people he wants us to be. We must remember to say 'thank you' for that as well, this harvest time.

*

Grandad's cereal box:
Ideas for classroom follow-up

RE

- The story of Moses, including the Ten Commandments, linking with NSNFRE themes of KS1: story, leaders and teachers; KS2: inspirational people, teachings and authority
- The Jewish festival of Pesach (Passover), its origins and contemporary celebration (KS1: celebration, symbols, believing; KS2: religion, family and community, worship, symbols of religious expression, beliefs and questions)

Geography

- Egypt

History, PSHE, RE, Citizenship

- Slavery and movements working for its abolition in the past and present in Britain, USA and so on: www.bbc.co.uk/history/british/abolition

Science

- The importance of an adequate and varied diet for general health and activity

English

- Create and act elements of the story of Moses, focusing on a variety of key characters—for example, Miriam, Pharaoh's daughter, Pharaoh, Aaron and Moses.
- Read the story of Moses and use it to fulfil elements of the English curriculum:
  - www.topmarks.co.uk/judaism/moses/moses1.htm
  - www.bbc.co.uk/religion/religions/judaism/history/moses_2.shtml (gives teachers the story and links through to information about Passover, the Ten Commandments and so on)
  - www.primaryresources.co.uk/re/docs/Moses_MB.doc (a fill-in-the-missing-words response to the story)

Art

- Look at Lorenzo Costa's *The Story of Moses (The Dance of Miriam)*:
  - www.nationalgallery.org.uk/paintings/lorenzo-costa-the-story-of-moses-the-dance-of-miriam

PE

- Inspired by the painting, devise a dance of celebration for freedom.

*

Section Two

The promised land

Key Bible verse

'Obey all the laws that I have given you today.
Then you will be able to cross the river and occupy the land
that you are about to enter.'
DEUTERONOMY 11:8–9

Values

Cooperation and perseverance

This section is designed to run from after the October break until the Christmas holiday. The theme is 'The promised land' and, in the big story of God's love for the world, we are remembering the time when his chosen people, the Israelites, were given a place of their own to live in. When we imagine ourselves within this part of the story, we learn about the need to work together with our friends to achieve challenging tasks. We also realise that God generously gives us what we need.

'The game of block-blast' is a story told in six parts plus a final episode at Christmas, which illustrates the biblical account of the conquest of the promised land and the way in which the Israelites settled and defended it. It is found at the end of the book of Deuteronomy and in the books of Joshua, Judges and Ruth.

- Week One: Deuteronomy 34
- Week Two: Joshua 6:1–21
- Week Three: Joshua 18:8–10; 21:43–45
- Week Four: Judges 4:4–16; 7:1–23

- **Week Five:** Judges 14—16
- **Week Six:** Ruth 4:11–17

The storyteller's prop used for 'The game of block-blast' consists of five large shapes made of foam off-cuts, which could all be of different colours, although they do not need to be.

- The 'stick': 30cm × 8cm × 8cm
- The 'fork': shaped like a tuning fork, with each straight part 8cm × 8cm thick
- The 'shield': 50cm square with a 5cm × 5cm hole in the middle
- The 'tree': a trunk measuring 61cm × 8cm × 8cm, with three short branches of length 13cm, 10cm and 8cm
- The 'cog': 50cm square with an 8cm wide 'slot' cut in from each of the four corners

These shapes are designed to be pieced together in various combinations. The foam should be 5–8cm thick (see overleaf).

Suggested music

Suggestions for pre-recorded music that could be used at the start and end of assemblies include:

- 'Joshua fit da battle of Jericho' (EMI Classical, B000002SNR)
- Music from the film *Gladiator* (Decca B00004STPT)

Suggestions for songs that could be sung at assemblies include:

- Father, we love you
- God's not dead, no!
- He's got the whole world in his hand
- I will enter his gates
- Jubilate!
- Make me a channel of your peace

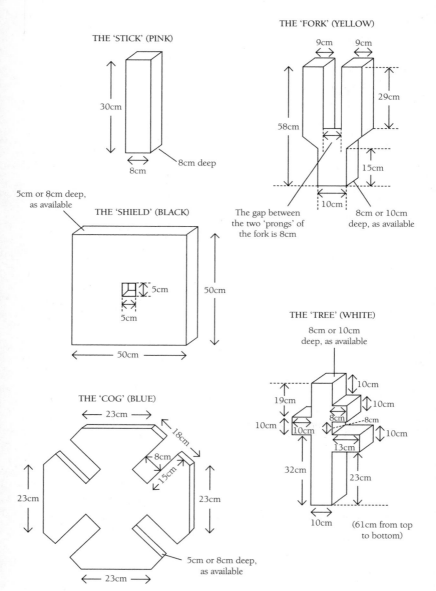

THE 'STICK' (PINK)

30cm

8cm

8cm deep

THE 'FORK' (YELLOW)

9cm   9cm

29cm

58cm

15cm

10cm

The gap between the two 'prongs' of the fork is 8cm

8cm or 10cm deep, as available

5cm or 8cm deep, as available

THE 'SHIELD' (BLACK)

5cm

50cm

5cm

50cm

THE 'TREE' (WHITE)

8cm or 10cm deep, as available

10cm

19cm

10cm

10cm   8cm

8cm

10cm

32cm

13cm

23cm

10cm

(61cm from top to bottom)

THE 'COG' (BLUE)

23cm

18cm

8cm

15cm

23cm

23cm

23cm

5cm or 8cm deep, as available

*

The game of block-blast: Week One

Bible link

This week's Bible passage link is Deuteronomy 34, which recounts the time when the Israelites prepared to enter the promised land and the death of Moses.

Key theme

This week's key theme is 'wanting to do our best' for someone we care about or someone who has helped us. Think about people who are important to us and how they have helped us. Consider how we could repay them and make them proud of us.

Episode One

(Have the five foam pieces to hand.)

I wonder if any of you enjoy playing sport. I wonder if you know what the most dangerous sport in the universe is. In fact, the most dangerous sport in the universe is called 'block-blast'. You've probably never heard of it, but today I want to start telling you a new story about one particular game of block-blast. It's a special story because it reminds us about God and about some things in the Bible.

First, I need to explain the rules of block-blast to you. There are seven players on each team, but there aren't just two teams: lots of teams can play a game of block-blast all at once. The pitch is like an enormous bowl, bigger than a normal football ground. In the middle of the pitch is a central 'base'. Lying all around the pitch are hundreds of big soft foam pieces, in five different shapes (*show the five foam shapes and name them: stick, fork, tree, shield, cog*). The teams playing block-blast are allowed to use these shapes to build weapons and defences (*show an example*).

Did I tell you how a team wins at block-blast? It's easy. All they have to do is capture and defend the base, keeping the other teams out, for one complete hour. It's just like a massive pillow-fight, but using the foam pieces. It's dangerous, but it's fun as well!

Once upon a time, the best game of block-blast that ever happened in the whole universe was played. It was for the Milky Way Cup, the trophy everyone wanted to win. Teams came from all over the universe to play. One of them was the Iron City team. Their captain was called Stella Steelfist and she was very strong. She loved making her favourite block-blast weapon out of the fork and the shield (*construct the weapon by pushing the single prong of the fork through the hole in the shield*). She could whack the opposition out of the way and defend herself easily (*allow a child to try swinging the weapon*). The rest of the team members were smaller than Stella and the smallest one of all was called Tiny Tron. He was the block-fetcher and his job was to fetch the foam shapes for his team-mates during the game.

The Iron City team had an amazing coach. His name was Plato and he was very old and wise. In fact, he was so old that his hair was completely white and he had to walk with a stick. Plato was so pleased with the team, because they'd made it to the final of the Milky Way Cup. None of his teams had ever done that before. Maybe this time his team would even win it.

When the day came for the match, Plato and the Iron City team got on to the space-bus so that they could fly from their home planet to the block-blast stadium. They made sure Plato was sitting next to the window and, as the space-bus flew over the ground, he smiled a big smile. It was the best pitch he'd ever seen. He realised he'd been looking forward to seeing it all his life, but the journey had made him tired and he shut his eyes.

When they landed, Stella Steelfist and the others tried to wake Plato up, but they could see that he was so old, he wouldn't ever wake up again. He had a lovely smile on his face, though, because the last thing he'd seen was the amazing stadium and the pitch. Tears came into Stella's eyes as she unpacked her bag from the space-bus. 'We must win the trophy as a thank-you to Plato,' she said to the rest of the Iron City team. 'We must work together better than we've ever done before.' The others all agreed as they started to get ready for the big game.

I haven't got time to tell you any more of my story today. Next time we'll hear what happened when the game began and we'll see what amazing things you can make out of the foam shapes. It's a very special story, because it reminds us of something in the Bible. Do you remember how Moses led the Israelites out of Egypt and through the wilderness? He was taking them to a place called the promised land, a country where God had promised his people could live. Moses came so close to that land, but the journey took so long that he was very old when they'd almost reached it. He even saw the promised land from a nearby mountain. He must have smiled when he saw it, but he died before he could actually go there, a bit like old Coach Plato, who saw the stadium from the space-bus but never actually made it there.

The Iron City team was just like the Israelites. They knew they had to capture the base in the middle of the stadium to win the game of block-blast and get the Milky Way trophy. And the Israelites knew they had to capture the promised land, the land that God wanted to give them.

I wonder if Stella Steelfist and the team will play well enough to win the game. Would you have enjoyed being in that team? I wonder if God's people will manage to take the land that he promised them. I wonder.

Possible concluding prayer

Lord God, you promised your people a place to live, a land full of milk and honey. When Moses was very old, you showed him the promised land before he died. Thank you for the good things you promise us, and help us to work together as a good team. Amen

*

The game of block-blast: Week Two

Bible link

This week's Bible passage link is Joshua 6:1–21, which recounts the time after Joshua and the Israelites had crossed the River Jordan into the promised land, when they attacked and captured the city of Jericho.

Key theme

This week's key theme is 'hurting others and getting hurt'. Does it matter about hurting other people? Think of different ways in which people can be hurt. Is it possible to go through life without being hurt or hurting others? Some sports are all about fighting and self-defence. What do you think about these kinds of sports? Think about the kinds of rules that are necessary in these sports.

Episode Two

(Have the five foam pieces to hand.)

Do you remember the story we began last time? What was the name of the most dangerous sport in the whole universe? Can you remember the names of the five foam shapes? *(Show the five foam shapes and name them: stick, fork, tree, shield, cog.)* Who was in the Iron City team, and what happened to their coach?

And do you remember how this story about the game called block-blast reminds us of the Israelites as they travelled to the promised land and how Moses died just before they reached it?

Stella Steelfist and the Iron City team had just made it to the stadium when suddenly the game began. There were loads of other teams playing and they all looked very good. Stella had to be the coach as well as the captain, so she called the team round. 'We must work together all the time,' she said. 'If we don't, we'll never win.' Then she sent Tiny Tron off to fetch some foam blocks.

Tiny Tron ran off to find them *(run through the names of the blocks: stick, fork, tree, shield, cog)*, but he could see that another team had grabbed the base already. They'd built high walls using different foam pieces, so the base was very well defended. In fact, he'd never seen such good walls before. 'How are we ever going to capture the base?' he asked himself. When he'd collected a big pile of foam shapes, he rushed back to the others to tell them.

Stella listened carefully. 'We'll have to attack them,' she said, as she started building an amazing weapon from the foam pieces *(construct a weapon using the foam shapes)*. Soon the others in the team were building weapons as well *(invite one of the children to build a different weapon)*. Now they were ready to attack!

Stella Steelfist and the team grabbed their weapons tightly. They ran round the outside of the base seven times, shouting as loudly as they could. Then they charged at the base and smashed their foam weapons into the walls. Stella Steelfist made sure they were working together, and, before long, the walls came tumbling down and the Iron City team were into the base. Their opponents on the other team ran away as fast as they could.

Stella and the team started doing high-fives and celebrating in the middle of the base. 'We've done it!' they shouted. But just then, Stella noticed Tiny Tron looking sad. 'Why do we have to do all this bashing and blasting?' he said. 'I don't understand it. People get hurt.' Stella was about to answer him when suddenly the match referee started talking on the loudspeakers, which were spread all round the stadium. His voice was very powerful. 'The Iron City team have grabbed the base,' he said, 'so now they just need to hold on to it for a complete hour—that's 60 minutes. I've started the countdown clock!'

Stella Steelfist and the others looked up at the clock, above the middle of the stadium. They could see the seconds counting down. 'Only 59 and a half minutes and we've won the Milky Way Cup!' they said to each other.

I haven't got time to tell you any more of my story today. Next time I'm sure we'll find out how long the Iron City team managed to hold the base. Do you remember how this story reminds us of the Israelites, who escaped from Egypt so that they could try to find the promised land, the land that God wanted to give them? Their leader, Moses, died before they got there, just like old Coach Plato in our story. But a new, younger leader called Joshua took over, just as Stella Steelfist took over as coach for the Iron City team. You can read about Joshua in the Bible. He helped the Israelites to work together as they invaded the land.

Joshua and the Israelites had to attack the cities that were already there, and one of them was called Jericho. It had big walls, just like the walls protecting the base in the game of block-blast. Joshua's men went round and round those walls at Jericho seven times, playing their trumpets as loudly as they could. It was just like Stella Steelfist and her team, who ran round the base seven times with their foam weapons, shouting and screaming. And the walls fell down! Joshua and the Israelites captured the promised land, just like Stella Steelfist and the Iron City team captured the base. But I wonder if there was anyone with Joshua who was like Tiny Tron, who asked why all the fighting had to happen?

Would you have been a good member of the Iron City team? What weapon would you have made out of the foam blocks? Would you have cooperated with Stella Steelfist and the others, to work well with them? I bet it was fun attacking the base and knocking the walls down! But what would you have said to Tiny Tron when he was sad?

I wonder what it was like being with Joshua and the Israelites when they attacked Jericho. They must have been very pleased when they captured the promised land. But I wonder if they thought the fighting was really a good thing. I wonder.

Possible concluding prayer

Lord God, you promised your people a place to live, a land full of milk and honey. You helped Joshua and the Israelites capture Jericho by making the walls tumble down. Thank you for the good things you promise us, and help us to work together as a good team. Amen

*

The game of block-blast: Week Three

Bible link

This week's Bible passage link is Joshua 18:8–10 and 21:43–45, which recounts the way in which God helped the Israelites divide the promised land between their tribes and how he promised to help them keep it.

Key theme

This week's key theme is 'working together as a team' and the different and important roles each member plays. Consider the teams the children are in and the parts they play. How important is it to work together to achieve success?

Episode Three

(Have the five foam pieces to hand.)

Do you remember our story from last time? Can you remember the names of the five foam shapes? *(Show the five foam shapes and name them: stick, fork, tree, shield, cog.)* Who was the captain of the Iron City team? Do you think Stella Steelfist and her team will be able to defend the base?

And do you remember how this story about the game called block-blast reminds us of Joshua and the Israelites, and how they captured Jericho and took the promised land?

Stella Steelfist and the others were excited that they'd captured the base. They wondered if they would even win the Milky Way

Cup. 'We need the best defences we've ever built,' said Stella to the others. 'This base has so many pathways leading in, and ropes you can swing on, it won't be easy to hold out for a whole hour. We'll have to work together and divide up the jobs evenly.'

Tiny Tron knew they would need loads of foam blocks, so he quickly ran out of the base to collect as many as he could. All the shapes would be useful, so he picked up a mixture of sticks and forks and trees and shields and cogs, and brought a massive pile back. Luckily, none of the other teams was ready to attack yet, but Stella knew it wouldn't be long. 'We must each build something different,' she said, and she quickly chose different jobs for each of them to do.

One of the team members started building tall walls using some shields and a few cogs. Someone else made clever trap-doors using some forks and a tree. Another person constructed some barriers made out of sticks and cogs, while a different person made a cunning dead end, so that the enemies would get stuck and a whole pile of every kind of foam block would come crashing down on them. Then one of the strongest members of the team designed an amazing new weapon using the foam shapes, a weapon that you could throw at an opponent (*invite one of the children to design a throwing weapon*).

After about ten minutes, they'd all finished and the defences were ready. The base looked very safe, but Stella and the others could hear shouts coming from outside the walls. 'We must all promise to do our best when an attack on the base begins,' said Stella to her team. They all nodded their heads, even Tiny Tron. But he was thinking inside, 'Why do we have to do all this bashing and blasting? I don't understand it. People get hurt.'

Just then, the referee's voice boomed around the stadium:

'The Iron City team have held the base for 15 minutes. Only another 45 to go and they will win the Cup!' Tiny Tron and the team started cheering, but suddenly their cheers were drowned out by a huge roar from outside the walls. They all froze, and, the next instant, a massive 'bomb' made from foam shapes came flying over the wall *(throw the foam weapon up in the air so it crashes down)*. Stella Steelfist lifted Tiny Tron up on her shoulders and he looked over the wall and saw...

I haven't got time to tell you any more of my story today. Next time we'll find out who threw that foam bomb over the walls. Do you remember how this story reminds us of the Israelites, who escaped from Egypt so that they could try to find the promised land, the land that God wanted to give them? Their leader was called Joshua, and soon they captured all the cities, including Jericho, just as the Iron City team captured the base in the game of block-blast.

Once Joshua and the Israelites had captured the promised land, they had to organise themselves so that they could defend it. They divided the land up between the twelve tribes of Israel, just as the Iron City team divided up all the tasks between them when they were building their defences. The Israelites had to work together and they had to remember that God had given them the land. So they built an altar to the Lord as well, and God promised to help them. It was a bit like when Stella Steelfist made the whole team promise to do their best. The other teams were getting ready to attack the base, and even the Israelites weren't completely safe. They had enemies who wanted to drive them out of the land they'd been given. But I wonder if there was anyone with Joshua who was like Tiny Tron and asked why all the fighting had to happen.

Would you have been a good member of the Iron City team? What defences would you have constructed out of the foam blocks? Would you have cooperated with Stella Steelfist and the others, to work well with them? I bet it was fun designing clever defences! But what would you have said to Tiny Tron when he was sad?

I wonder what it was like being with Joshua and the Israelites when they organised the promised land so that each tribe had their own special place. They must have been very pleased to have a home of their own, but I wonder if they thought the fighting was really a good thing. I wonder.

Possible concluding prayer

Lord God, you promised your people a place to live, a land full of milk and honey, and they shared the land between them so that they could defend it well. Thank you for the good things you promise us, and help us to work together as a good team. Amen

*

The game of block-blast: Week Four

Bible link

This week's Bible passage link is Judges 4:4–16 and 7:1–23, which recounts the times when the Canaanites and Midianites attacked the Israelites and when Deborah and Gideon defeated them to keep the promised land safe.

Key theme

This week's key theme is 'fighting vs peace'. Our story is about a game, but in real-life situations people disagree about whether it is right to fight—in the playground or in wars. Explore ideas about when pupils think it might be acceptable to fight, and ideas about pacifism.

Episode Four

(Have the five foam pieces to hand.)

Do you remember our story from last time? Can you remember the names of the five foam shapes? (*Show the five foam shapes and name them: stick, fork, tree, shield, cog.*) What did Stella Steelfist and the team do to make the base safe? Do you think they will win the Milky Way Cup?

And do you remember how this story about the game called block-blast reminds us of the Israelites? They conquered the promised land, and then Joshua organised them so that they could defend it well.

The shouts out in the stadium were getting louder. Stella Steelfist lifted Tiny Tron up so that he could just see over the top of the walls. He was wondering who had thrown the foam bomb into the base, but when he looked he couldn't stop himself yelling in terror. 'Help! It's an attack!' he screamed. One of the other teams, called the Cane Trains, had lined up its members and they all had their favourite team weapon, made from a fork and a cog *(make the weapon by pushing the double prongs of the fork into opposite slots of the cog)*. They were waving their weapons around fiercely above their heads and yelling a terrifying scream. Then they charged forward.

The Iron City team did their best to fight back, but they seemed to be losing. Just then, Stella Steelfist remembered an amazing weapon she'd made out of the foam blocks and hidden behind a wall in the base. It was a very clever design *(invite one of the children to create a weapon)*. When Stella had found the weapon, she ran out from the base, swinging it above her head. She was all ready to fight as hard as she could, but the Cane Trains could see what a frightening weapon it was. They got in a panic just at the sight of it, and, before Stella could come any closer, they'd all run away as fast as they could.

The Iron City team cheered in triumph. They'd defended the base. Their enemy had run away. They were just relaxing when they heard another roar from outside the walls. Tiny Tron poked his head up again to see who was there this time. 'It's another attack!' he screamed. 'It's even worse than before!' This time it was a dangerous enemy called the Midnight Monsters team. Their special weapon was made from a tree and a stick *(make the weapon by slotting the middle of the stick in between the two arms of the tree)*. The whole team had two of them each, and they were whirling them around above their heads. Suddenly the enemies all ran forward with a whooping sound, which made Stella and the others feel very frightened. Before long, everyone was whacking their enemies using the foam weapons.

The battle wasn't going well, but Tiny Tron had an idea. He quickly made a special throwing weapon, using a very clever design *(invite one of the children to create a weapon)*. Then he swung it round a few times and threw it right into the middle of the Midnight Monsters team. They were caught by surprise. They thought one of their own team had attacked them, so they started fighting each other and, before long, they'd all run away.

Stella Steelfist and the others tried to cheer again, but they were completely exhausted, especially Tiny Tron. He was thinking to himself sadly, 'Why do we have to do all this bashing and blasting? I don't understand it. People get hurt.' But at that very moment the referee's voice echoed around the stadium again: 'No one has taken the base yet, and the Iron City team have held it for 30 minutes now. They're halfway to the Cup!' Before they could celebrate, Stella Steelfist and the others heard something else that sent a shiver down their backs. It made them very worried indeed. They could hear the war-chant of the deadliest team in the whole galaxy...

I haven't got time to tell you any more of my story today. Maybe next time we'll find out which was the deadliest team and whether Stella and her team survived. Do you remember how this story reminds us of the Israelites and how they had to defend the promised land? The Iron City team had to fight off the Cane Trains and the Midnight Monsters, and the Israelites had to fight two great enemies—the Canaanites and the Midianites. A person called Deborah defeated the Canaanites (they got in a panic) and a person called Gideon defeated the Midianites (they attacked the members of their own army). It was just like when the Iron City team defeated the Cane Trains and the Midnight Monsters. You can read about Deborah and Gideon in the Bible. But I wonder if there was anyone like Tiny Tron, who was frightened of all the fighting and didn't like it?

If you'd been in the Iron City team, would you have been brave enough to fight the enemy off? What weapon would you have made? Would you have remembered to work together with Stella Steelfist and the others in your team? And what would you have said to Tiny Tron when he was sad?

I wonder what it was like being with the Israelites when they had to fight the Canaanites and the Midianites. They must have been relieved when their enemies ran away and the base was safe, but I wonder if they thought the fighting was really a good thing. I wonder.

Possible concluding prayer

Lord God, you promised your people a place to live, a land full of milk and honey. You helped them work together to defend themselves and made their enemies run away. Thank you for the good things you promise us, and help us to work together as a good team. Amen

*

The game of block-blast: Week Five

Bible link

This week's Bible passage link is Judges 14—16, which recounts the time when Samson fought against the Philistines.

Key theme

This week's key theme is 'tricks'. Tricks can be fun and funny or they can be serious and hurtful. Consider these different aspects of tricks. Think about how what one person thinks is a funny trick can upset someone else. Consider the consequences of such actions, and our responses and responsibilities.

Episode Five

(Have the five foam pieces to hand.)

Do you remember our story from last time? Can you remember the names of the five foam shapes? (*Show the five foam shapes and name them: stick, fork, tree, shield, cog.*) Which two teams did Stella Steelfist and the team defeat to keep the base safe? Do you think they will win the Milky Way Cup?

And do you remember how this story about the game called block-blast reminds us of the Israelites? They defended the promised land against all their enemies, including the Canaanites and Midianites.

The Iron City team were very tired by now, but their captain, Stella Steelfist, tried to encourage them. 'Only another 30 minutes and we'll have won the trophy,' she said. But just as she spoke, they all heard a terrifying noise. It was the war cry of the deadliest team in the whole galaxy—the Flame Stone team. Tiny Tron looked out over the walls and knew straight away that it was hopeless trying to fight them. 'They're invincible!' he squeaked with a frightened voice. 'We must run away!'

The Flame Stone team always used extra-big weapons made from the foam blocks *(make a weapon using all five shapes)*. Soon they were next to the walls, starting to break through. Suddenly Stella Steelfist had an idea. She grabbed hold of Tiny Tron and whispered in his ear, 'Why don't you climb on my shoulders, and I'll tie you on with string. Then you'll be the tallest person in the whole stadium. We'll make the best whacking weapon that's ever been built, so you can beat the enemy back. I'll carry you and we can work together.' Tiny Tron shook his head. He was terrified—it sounded so dangerous—but in the end Stella persuaded him. Quickly they built the best whacking weapon they could out of the foam blocks *(invite a child to make a weapon)*. Then Tiny Tron jumped up on Stella's shoulders.

At just that moment, the final Flame Stone attack began. Luckily, Stella Steelfist and Tiny Tron were ready. Tiny Tron wasn't tiny any more! He was taller than anyone else and he whacked as hard as he could with his weapon. Three times the enemy attacked and three times he beat them back. 'Maybe we really will win,' thought Tiny Tron to himself, but just then, something dreadful happened. One of the Flame Stone warriors shouted, 'Watch out! The wall behind you is collapsing!' Stella and Tiny Tron looked round, but the wall was fine. It was a trick! One of the enemy rushed up behind them and cut the string holding Tiny Tron in place on Stella's shoulders. He fell off with a crash and, in an instant, he'd been captured.

Quickly the Flame Stone team brought Tiny Tron to the gate, holding him tightly. 'We've won now!' they were shouting. Stella and the others had tears in their eyes. They so wanted to win the trophy, but now they were about to lose the base. Tiny Tron had tears in his eyes as well, but, as he stopped under the gate, which was made of all sorts of foam shapes, he had an idea. In a flash, he'd wriggled free and was pushing as hard as he could against the pillars of the gate. Harder and harder he pushed until the whole gate came crashing down *(shower foam shapes down on to the floor)*. The Flame Stones were taken by surprise. They fell down under the shower of blocks. Stella Steelfist and the Iron City team ran up and beat them out of the base with a cheer. But Tiny Tron was thinking to himself sadly, 'Why do we have to do all this bashing and blasting? I don't understand it. People get hurt.'

Just then, the referee's voice could be heard. 'The Iron City team have held the base for 50 minutes now. Only another ten to go...'

I haven't got time to tell you any more of my story today. Next time we'll find out if Stella and her team really did win the trophy. But do you remember how this story reminds us of how the Israelites had to defend the promised land? The Iron City team had to fight off the Flame Stones, and the Israelites had to fight a mighty enemy called the Philistines. The Philistines kept attacking, but a massive Israelite with long hair, called Samson, beat them off. It was just like when Tiny Tron made himself massive by standing on Stella's shoulders. The Flame Stones tricked Tiny Tron, and the Philistines tricked Samson.

They cut off his hair to make him weak and they captured him, just as Tiny Tron was captured. Then, Samson managed to use his strength one last time to make a building collapse, which destroyed the Philistines, just as Tiny Tron defeated the Flame Stone team by making the gate collapse.

If you'd been Tiny Tron, would you have stood on Stella's shoulders? Would you have made the gate collapse? Would you have been sad about all the bashing?

I wonder what it was like being with Samson and the Israelites when they had to fight the Philistines. They must have been pleased when the enemy was defeated and the promised land was safe. But I wonder if they thought the fighting was really a good thing. I wonder.

Possible concluding prayer

Lord God, you promised your people a place to live, a land full of milk and honey. You made Samson so brave, even when the enemy tricked him, and he kept the promised land safe. Thank you for the good things you promise us, and help us to work together as a good team. Amen

*

The game of block-blast: Week Six

Bible link

This week's Bible passage link is Ruth 4:11–17, which recounts the way in which one of the families in the promised land, who lived in Bethlehem, gave rise to King David and, eventually, another even more important king.

Key theme

This week's key theme is 'winning'. Explore feelings associated with winning—for example, excitement, pride, achievement, happiness, elation and exhaustion. Is the effort worthwhile? Consider whether winning at any cost is acceptable. What if Tiny Tron had been taken prisoner, held hostage or injured?

Episode Six

(Have the five foam pieces to hand.)

Do you remember our story from last time? Can you remember the names of the five foam shapes? *(Show the five foam shapes and name them: stick, fork, tree, shield, cog.)* How did Stella and the team defend the base against their fiercest enemy? Do you think they'll win the Milky Way Cup?

And do you remember how this story about the game called block-blast reminds us of Samson and the Israelites? They defended the promised land against all their enemies, including the Philistines.

'Only ten minutes to go,' the referee shouted through his loudspeaker. Stella Steelfist and the Iron City team looked at each other in excitement. 'We're going to do it!' screamed Stella, but she knew inside her that the last ten minutes in a game of block-blast are always the hardest. She knew that all the other teams would keep attacking. She knew the Iron City team would have to work together better than ever before.

Tiny Tron raced out of the base, looking for as many shield foam blocks as he could find. He found plenty and the team grabbed them so that they were ready. 'Look!' shouted Stella. 'Here comes an enemy!' It was a team carrying tree blocks, and they ran towards the base with glinting eyes *(ask a small child to try to bash through using the tree while you hold them back using the shield)*. But the defences held firm. A minute later, another team of enemies came swinging in using ropes and carrying fork blocks *(ask another small child to try to bash through using the fork while you hold them back using the shield)*. Stella and her team held them back, even though the fighting was tougher than ever.

No sooner had one enemy gone than another arrived. Next, it was a team who marched in a line, all carrying stick blocks *(ask another small child to try to bash through using the stick while you hold them back using the shield)*. But the Iron City team was too strong. No one could get past them. The base was safe.

Tiny Tron looked up at the clock. 'There's only one minute left!' he shouted in triumph. The referee started the final countdown: 'Ten, nine, eight...' Tiny Tron's heart was beating quickly. Could it be true? They were going to win the trophy! '... seven, six, five, four, three, two, one...' Then the whistle was blown. 'Yes!' yelled Stella Steelfist and Tiny Tron together. 'Yes! We've done it!' They were jumping around with excitement.

Quickly Stella gathered the team around. 'This is a special moment,' she said. 'Remember it for the rest of your lives and tell your friends and families. Coach Plato would be proud of us.' Just then, the Galactic President of the Block-Blast Federation appeared with the Milky Way Cup. 'Who's going to receive the trophy?' asked Stella. They all looked at Tiny Tron. 'You must have it,' she said. 'We couldn't have done it without you.' So Tiny Tron took the cup in his hands and held it up high. The whole stadium roared with a massive cheer! He had his eyes shut now, and he was imagining keeping it very safely. 'I'll hand it down to my children and my grandchildren and their children, and so on,' he was thinking to himself.

Then he imagined a day, a long time in the future, when one of his family would find the Milky Way Cup and would ask about it: 'Who won this? Was it the best game of block-blast ever?' Tiny Tron smiled a big smile. Maybe that person in his family, a long time in the future, would go on to become the best block-blast player ever in the history of the universe—a player so good that no one would ever even try to battle against them.

As Tiny Tron opened his eyes again, he realised why all the bashing and blasting had to happen. It was worth it, because that person in his family would be the king of block-blast.

Our story is almost finished now, and I'm sure you remember that it reminds us about God and things in the Bible. The game of block-blast, which the Iron City team won, reminds us of how the Israelites held the promised land for many years. Tiny Tron kept the Milky Way Cup in his family for generations, carefully handed down, and in the Bible we can read about a person called Ruth who lived in the promised land. She got married and had children and grandchildren and so on.

In the end, one of Tiny Tron's descendants was a block-blast player so good that no one even tried to battle him, which made all the bashing worthwhile. And in the end, one of Ruth's descendants was a king so good that he was even called the 'King of kings'. All the fighting that the people of God had to do to keep the promised land was worth it, so that this king could be born.

I wonder if any of you know who that king was. I'm not going to tell you, but I'll give you a clue. Ruth came from a special place in the promised land, the land that God gave to his people and helped them defend. The name of that place was Bethlehem.

Possible concluding prayer

Lord God, you promised your people a place to live, a land full of milk and honey. In that land was a town called Bethlehem, a place where kings were born. Thank you for sending us the 'King of kings' and for showing us how much you love us. Amen

*

The game of block-blast:
Concluding celebration

The story of 'The game of block-blast' ends with a Christmas celebration. You could plan a nativity play or a more traditional carol service, or use this final episode separately. The concluding episode of the story reminds us that Bethlehem was in the promised land and Jesus was born there.

Key theme

This week's key theme is Christmas. There are many themes that it would be appropriate to pursue—for example, Jesus as the second Adam, incarnation, or the nativity narrative.

Concluding episode

Do you remember what these five foam shapes are used for? Can you remember their names? (*Show the five foam shapes and name them, making sure the tree is last: stick, fork, shield, cog, tree.*) Although the game of block-blast sounded great fun, it's only a story—but it's a story that reminds us of some important things in the Bible.

The game of block-blast helped us learn about God's people, the Israelites, and about the promised land they were given. Just like the game in our story, the battles fought by the Israelites were very fierce. They had to fight the Canaanites and the Midianites and the Philistines. Sometimes we wonder if all that fighting was really needed, just like Tiny Tron in our story, who kept wondering if all the bashing and blasting was really needed.

But in the end we found out why it was. We discovered about a special place in the promised land, a place called Bethlehem.

(Show the tree shape.) The prophets said that the promised land was a bit like a tree. Although it grew strong and lived a long time, in the end this tree was chopped down: the promised land was eventually captured by even more powerful enemies. The prophets also said that the tree would sprout up again. They said it would grow again in Bethlehem. It might seem strange, but that tree is actually part of the Christmas story, because Jesus was the person the prophets were talking about. He was born in Bethlehem and his birth is what we celebrate at Christmas.

The tree that the prophets talked about, at Bethlehem, isn't the only tree in the Bible. Can you think of another one? There's a tree right at the start of the Bible, in the garden of Eden *(show the tree shape again)*. It was a tree with an apple on it, which God told Adam not to eat. Adam disobeyed God. He took the apple and ate it, and then everything went wrong. Someone very special was needed to put things right again. Did you know that Jesus is sometimes called the 'Second Adam', because he was the only person who could reverse the mistake that Adam made? Things went wrong after Adam's mistake, but, when Jesus came, everything was set to go right again. So it might seem strange, but the tree in the garden of Eden is actually part of the Christmas story. Only Jesus could undo the mistake of that tree, and that's what we celebrate at Christmas as well.

So far, I've talked about two trees in the Bible. One was the tree the prophets knew about, which had been chopped down but would grow again in Bethlehem. The second tree was the one Adam picked the apple from. But there's another tree as well. It's called the 'tree of shame', and it was shaped like a cross *(show the tree shape again)*. It was the tree where Jesus died. That was a very sad day, but it was a very special day as well. It was the day when God showed us how much he loved us, because Jesus was willing to give up everything for us, even his life. Jesus couldn't have done that unless he'd been born in Bethlehem many years earlier. So it might seem strange, but the 'tree of shame' is actually part of the Christmas story. Only Jesus could give his life for us, and that's what we celebrate at Christmas as well.

So far, I've talked about three trees in the Bible. One was the tree the prophets knew about, which had been chopped down but would grow again at Bethlehem. The second tree was the one Adam picked the apple from, and the third tree was the one shaped like a cross, where Jesus gave his life because he loved us so much. But there's another tree in the Bible as well. It comes right at the end. It's called the 'tree of life' *(show the tree shape again)*. It brings peace and healing, which is what God has promised will happen in the end. Jesus brings peace and healing to the earth. That was what the angels told the shepherds. Jesus makes the 'tree of life' real for us already. So it might seem strange, but the tree of life, which brings peace and healing, is actually part of the Christmas story as well. When Jesus was born in Bethlehem, he brought peace to earth, and that's one of the most important things we celebrate at Christmas.

So when you see this tree shape *(show the shape again)*, try to remember the story of the game of block-blast. Try to remember the story of how the Israelites defended the promised land. Try to remember about Bethlehem, that special place in the promised land, and how the prophets said that a new tree would spring up there. Try to remember about Adam's tree and how Jesus put right his mistake. Try to remember about the 'tree of shame', which was where Jesus showed how much he loved us. And try to remember about the 'tree of life' and how Jesus brings peace and healing to the earth.

If you can remember all of those trees, you will really have understood what Christmas is all about.

*

The game of block-blast:
Ideas for classroom follow-up

RE

- Read the stories of Joshua, Deborah, Gideon, Samson and Ruth.
- Study Judaism and Jewish celebrations: for example, explore the Jewish festival of Shavuoth, during which the story of Ruth is read.
- Familiarise young children with the nativity narrative, perhaps organising a nativity play. Older pupils can consider the trees talked about in the final episode of the story (which might involve a revision of the story of Adam and Eve in Genesis 3) and the new covenant between God and humankind made through Jesus.

Music

- Learn to sing the song 'Joshua fought the battle of Jericho'. YouTube has several film clips of choirs performing this song. For example, see www.youtube.com/watch?v=H4znSPpeAjM

History

- Explore weapons and defences in relation to particular periods of history.
- Read about an example of a 'trick'—the Trojan Horse.
- What do we know about our own family histories? (Caution: consideration needs to be given to children in care, fostering or adoption situations.)

History, PSHE, RE

- Explore the idea of pacifism and examples of people who have practised it—for example, The Society of Friends (or Quakers) and conscientious objectors in war time.

*

Section Three

The disciples of Jesus

Key Bible verse

Jesus said, 'Whoever wants to serve me must follow me.'
JOHN 12:26

Values

Friendship and exploration

This section is designed to run from January until the February break. The theme is 'The disciples of Jesus' and, in the big story of God's love for the world, we are remembering the close friends that Jesus had and the way they followed him but made mistakes as well. When we imagine ourselves within this part of the story, we discover how hard it is to follow Jesus and how important true friendship is.

'The pioneer's drum' is a story told in six parts, plus a concluding episode, which illustrates the biblical account of how the disciples were called to follow Jesus, what he asked them to do and how they deserted him. This account is set out vividly in Mark's Gospel.

- Week One: Mark 1:16–20
- Week Two: Mark 5:25–34; 6:35–44
- Week Three: Mark 4:35–41
- Week Four: Mark 8:31–35
- Week Five: Mark 10:35–45
- Week Six: Mark 6:7–12; 14:27–31

The storyteller's prop used for 'The pioneer's drum' consists of:

- A drum, which could be made from an upturned biscuit or chocolate tin, suitably decorated and incorporating a shoulder strap, with the words 'The pioneer's drum' on it
- Two drumsticks

Suggested music

Suggestions for prerecorded music that could be used at the start and end of assemblies include:

- African Drums (Madou Djembé, Playasound Airmail B00006IWD5)
- African Sanctus (David Fanshawe, Classics B000025AXD)

Suggestions for songs that could be sung at assemblies include:

- A new commandment
- Follow me
- Give thanks with a grateful heart
- Glory to God (Peruvian Gloria) accompanied by drums
- Lord Jesus Christ (Living Lord)
- Will you come and follow me?

*

The pioneer's drum: Week One

Bible link

This week's Bible passage link is Mark 1:16–20, which recounts the way in which Jesus asked fishermen called Simon, Andrew, James and John to follow him and help him in his mission.

Key theme

This week's key theme is 'following'. Why do people choose to follow others? What qualities might a person need in order to persuade others to follow them? Why might it be important to be cautious about following someone who seems special? Another theme is 'things that keep us going'. The story starts with a hidden water source that irrigates the village. What things do we have in our lives that keep us going and enrich our lives, making them interesting, enjoyable, happy and so on?

Episode One

(Have the drum and drumsticks to hand.)

Today I want to start telling a new story. It's about a man who was a carpenter and lived in a village in a dry and dusty country. Although the countryside all around the village was like a desert, the village itself had plenty of lovely green grass and all the plants there grew really well. Everything was green and lush.

Even though the village had so many beautiful plants, the people there still grumbled all the time. They grumbled that it was too hot or too cold, or they even grumbled about each other. In fact, the carpenter was the only one who didn't grumble. He was too busy making tables and doors and all the other wooden things that people needed.

One day, the carpenter got so fed up with hearing everyone grumbling that he stood in the middle of the village and reminded them how lucky they were. 'Look!' he said. 'The ground here is so damp, everything grows well—not like out in the countryside where it's dry. Why are you grumbling? You're very lucky! Our water is a gift. It comes from an underground river.' But the people didn't believe him. 'We've never seen this river!' they shouted at him, and they carried on grumbling.

This made the carpenter very sad. It made him want to find the river for himself and discover its source, the place where it started. Quickly he started building a boat, strong enough to survive a long journey. He made a little cabin in the boat and a rudder to steer with, and, of course, some paddles to make it go. People in the village came to look. They laughed at him, but the carpenter kept working until the boat was finished. Then he scratched his head. 'How am I going to find the river, deep underground?' he wondered.

Just then, a mysterious old woman stopped in front of his workshop. She was wearing a long cloak and she asked the carpenter what the boat was for. So the man explained and straight away the old woman pulled out from her cloak a crinkly old map. 'This will help you find a way to the river and to its source,' she said. Before the carpenter could thank her, she pulled something else from her cloak (*show the drum and drumsticks*). 'These will be useful as well,' she smiled.

The carpenter read the words written on the side: 'The pioneer's drum'. Then he put it over his shoulder and tried it out *(play the drum)*. It made a wonderful noise. 'Maybe I'm the pioneer,' he said to himself. He looked up, but the mysterious old woman had disappeared. Quickly he looked at the map she'd given him. It showed a secret passageway leading down to the river, so the pioneer ran to look for himself. He could hear the noise of the water flowing. 'All I have to do is get my boat down there and I'll be on my way,' he laughed, but the boat was too heavy! However hard he tried, he couldn't move it. Exhausted, he sat down on the ground, but then he noticed the drum again. He picked up the drumsticks and started walking through the village, beating a special rhythm on the drum. *(Play the rhythm of 'Will you come and follow me?'.)* After a few minutes, some people came out of their houses. 'Why are you beating that rhythm?' they asked.

So the pioneer explained his plan to find the source of the river. 'Come with me!' he said. 'Come and follow me and we'll find the source of the river, which makes our village so green and alive.' Most of the people shook their heads and went back to their jobs, but a few decided they would come and help him move the boat. They were interested in seeing the river.

I haven't got time to tell you any more of our story today, but next time we'll hear what happened when the pioneer's new friends followed him. I wonder if you know what a pioneer really is. A pioneer is someone who leads the way and does things that no one else has ever done before. This story reminds us of someone in the Bible who was a pioneer. Can you guess who he was? The pioneer is Jesus, and he shows people the way to find God.

In our story, the pioneer played his drum using a special rhythm *(play the rhythm of 'Will you come and follow me?')*, and he asked the people in the village to come with him. It was the same when Jesus asked people to come with him. The first four were fishermen and Jesus asked them to come and follow him so that they could start fishing for people. Jesus wanted to show people that the source of their life came from God, while the pioneer in our story wanted to show people the source of the river that gave life. The pioneer needed friends to help him and Jesus looked for friends to help him as well. They were his disciples.

If you'd been living in the village and heard the pioneer playing his drum (*play the rhythm of 'Will you come and follow me?' again*), would you have followed him? If Jesus had asked you to follow him with the disciples, would you have gone and left everything behind? I wonder.

Possible concluding prayer

Lord God, thank you that Jesus was a pioneer who did things no one else had ever done before. Thank you that Jesus had friends who came with him to help him. Thank you also for our friends, and help us to be good friends to others. Amen

*

The pioneer's drum: Week Two

Bible link

This week's Bible passage links are Mark 5:25–34 and 6:35–44, which recount times when Jesus healed a woman and gave a hungry crowd food, even though his disciples were worried about what he was doing.

Key theme

This week's key theme is 'helping others'. Think about why it is important to help others, how we can help others and how others help us. What part can we play in helping people who are sick or hungry? Pupils might be preparing ideas for what they can do for Comic Relief after the February break. With those who are able, it might be possible to explore the idea of physical hunger as a metaphor and how other 'hungers' can be helped and satisfied.

Episode Two

(Have the drum and drumsticks to hand.)

Do you remember the story we began last time? What was unusual about the village? Who played this rhythm on the drum? *(Play the rhythm of 'Will you come and follow me?'.)* What did it mean and what was the pioneer hoping to find?

Do you remember how this story about the pioneer's drum reminds us of Jesus and his disciples? They decided to follow him so that they could find out more about God.

The pioneer showed his new friends the map and, in no time, they'd carried the boat down the secret passageway to the underground river. 'It's beautiful!' they cried, and they splashed their hands and feet in the cool, fresh water. Quickly they launched the boat into the river and got the paddles ready. 'I wonder how far it is to the source of this river,' said the pioneer. 'It must be miles away.' But no one worried. They were too excited as they set off.

Before long, the paddles were dipping in the water and the boat raced forward. The pioneer started beating a rhythm on his drum. (*Invite a child to beat a rhythm.*) Soon they could see sunlight up ahead and, in another instant, they had come bursting out of the underground tunnel into a deep ravine. Still they paddled on, but when they came around the next corner they were surprised to see a small settlement beside the river. 'Let's stop here for a rest,' said the pioneer's friends, but, as they paddled closer, they could see that something was wrong.

The people in the settlement were sitting on the ground. They had flies buzzing around them and they looked very ill. 'We can't stop here!' shouted the pioneer's friends. 'There's nothing we can do to help them and it wouldn't be safe.' But the pioneer was steering the boat towards the settlement and, as they reached the riverside, he stepped right into the middle of the ill people. Then he started beating a new rhythm on his drum. (*Play the rhythm of 'When I needed a neighbour'.*) Gradually the people started smiling as they listened, and before long they had jumped up and were dancing. The pioneer's friends were amazed. He had cured them! Then his rhythm changed back to the one they'd first heard. (*Play the rhythm of 'Will you come and follow me?'.)* 'Come and follow me,' said the pioneer, and some of the healed people leapt on to the boat.

On they paddled again *(beat a rhythm on the drum)* and, after another couple of hours, they reached another settlement, even smaller than the last one. The people there were crowded along the bank of the river. 'Help us!' they were calling weakly. 'We're starving! We need food!' The pioneer's friends were very worried. 'We haven't got enough food to share with them,' they muttered, so they pushed their paddles against the riverbank to try to escape. But the pioneer steered the boat to the side and jumped off with his drum. In an instant he was playing a new rhythm *(play the rhythm of 'I am the bread of life')* and the hungry people all gathered round. Somehow there seemed to be enough food for everyone to eat, and the crowd was shouting for joy. The pioneer had fed all the people. His friends were amazed.

Quickly he jumped back in the boat and off they went again. *(Beat a rhythm.)* His friends were asking each other how the pioneer could do these things. 'I think it's the river,' said one of them. 'It gives life to our village and it gives life to everyone if the pioneer is there. I'm pleased we came with him when he called us.'

On they paddled, but soon the drumbeat stopped. The pioneer had fallen asleep. His friends kept as quiet as possible but suddenly they heard a rumbling sound up ahead—the sound of thunder...

I haven't got time to tell you any more of our story today. Next time we'll find out what happened to the pioneer and his friends. Do you remember how this story reminds us of Jesus? He was a pioneer—someone who does things that no one else has ever done before. He shows people the way to find God.

In our story, the pioneer used his drum when he called people to follow him. *(Play the rhythm of 'Will you come and follow me?'.)* He also used his drum when he was helping people who were ill *(play the rhythm of 'When I needed a neighbour')* and helping people who were hungry *(play the rhythm of 'I am the bread of life')*. The pioneer's friends were worried, and it was the same when Jesus helped people who were ill and hungry. His disciples were worried. They didn't understand what Jesus was doing. Jesus wanted to show people that the source of their life came from God, and the pioneer in our story wanted to show people the source of the river that gave life.

If you'd been one of the pioneer's friends, would you have enjoyed hearing him playing his drum? *(Play the rhythm of 'Will you come and follow me?' again.)* Would you have been worried about the ill and hungry people? If you'd been one of Jesus' disciples, would you have been worried when he started healing people and giving them your food? I wonder.

Possible concluding prayer

Lord God, thank you that Jesus was a pioneer who did things no one else had ever done before. Sometimes the friends of Jesus were worried when he helped the sick and hungry people. Please help us not to be worried, and help us to be good friends to others. Amen

*

The pioneer's drum: Week Three

Bible link

This week's Bible passage link is Mark 4:35–41, which recounts the time when Jesus calmed the storm on the lake, when his disciples lacked faith in God and were amazed at his power.

Key theme

This week's key theme is 'storms of life'. Everyone has times when they are afraid and worried—not just in stormy weather. Who or what do we turn to, to help and comfort us in these times? How can we comfort and support others?

Episode Three

(Have the drum and drumsticks to hand.)

Do you remember our story from last time? What are the pioneer and his friends looking for? What did this rhythm on the drum mean *(play the rhythm of 'Will you come and follow me?')* and what were the pioneer's friends so worried about?

Do you remember how this story about the pioneer's drum reminds us of Jesus and his disciples? They decided to follow him so that they could find out more about God.

The pioneer had fallen asleep in the boat and his drum was silent. His friends kept on paddling quietly but the sky above was getting darker. They could hear the rumble of thunder in the distance. *(Make a gentle rumbling sound using the drum.)* Gradually it got louder and louder *(make a louder rumble)*, but still the pioneer was fast asleep. Suddenly a great flash of lightning filled the sky and a massive roll of thunder echoed in the river valley. *(Make a very loud and long rumble.)* A strong wind started blowing and waves splashed up over the edge of the boat.

The pioneer's friends tried to paddle over to the riverbank but the wind and the waves made it impossible. They couldn't believe it, but the pioneer was still fast asleep in the back of the boat, with the drum tucked under his arm. 'We must wake him up!' yelled someone, but he looked so peaceful that they didn't want to disturb him. Just then, an even bigger wave splashed over the side, making everyone soaking wet. Even the pioneer had water dripping off his clothes, but still he was asleep. One of the pioneer's friends grabbed the drum and gave it a tug. 'Don't you care that we're all about to drown?' he shouted as he shook the pioneer awake.

In an instant, the pioneer was standing up, looking at the waves and the dark sky, listening to the roaring wind. He didn't seem to be frightened at all. Then he started playing the drum, using a new rhythm that his friends hadn't heard before. *(Play the rhythm of 'Be still, for the presence of the Lord'.)* First he played it softly, then he played it again with a louder beat. *(Play the rhythm of 'Be still, for the presence of the Lord' again.)* The wind started dying down and the waves turned into tiny ripples. The clouds melted away, leaving lovely sunshine in their place. Still the pioneer was playing his new rhythm, softly again now. *(Play the rhythm of 'Be still, for the presence of the Lord' again.)*

'Why were you afraid?' asked the pioneer. 'Don't you believe that the river gives life?' His friends didn't know what to say.

They couldn't believe that the pioneer's drum had stopped the storm. Slowly they paddled onwards and the pioneer beat out a rhythm to help them keep in time. (*Beat a rhythm on the drum.*) It was getting late now, so they pulled over to the riverbank and tied up the boat. It was the perfect place for a camp.

After a while, the pioneer said that he was going off to be quiet, alone. When he'd gone, his friends started talking together. 'I don't know which was the most amazing thing I've seen,' said one of the group. 'The pioneer has healed sick people and fed hungry people and now he's even made the storm stop. The river seems to give him an amazing power when he plays his drum. Just think what we'll be able to tell the people back at the village when we return.'

Just then, another one of the pioneer's friends suddenly jumped up, holding the map. 'We can't go on any more tomorrow,' he exclaimed in a worried voice. 'It's too dangerous. I've been looking at the map and I've seen...'

Well, I haven't got time to tell you any more of our story today. Next time we might find out what lay ahead on the river, but do you remember how this story reminds us of Jesus? He was a pioneer—someone who does things that no one else has ever done before. He shows people the way to find God.

In our story, the pioneer used his drum to make the storm die down and the waves stop. (*Play the rhythm of 'Be still, for the presence of the Lord'.*) His friends were amazed, and that was just what it was like one time when Jesus was in a boat with his disciples. They were crossing over a lake when a storm struck. Their boat was about to sink but Jesus was asleep. His disciples were so worried that they woke him up, and then Jesus amazed them by making the storm and the waves stop. Jesus asked his disciples, 'Why were you afraid? Don't you have any faith?' They found it hard to believe the power he had. Jesus wanted to show them that the source of his power was God, and the pioneer in our story wanted to show people the source of the river that gave life.

If you'd been one of the pioneer's friends, would you have been frightened by the storm? (*Play a rumble on the drum.*) Would you have woken the pioneer up? If you'd been one of the disciples with Jesus, would you have believed he could calm the storm? Would you have trusted in God's power that much? I wonder.

Possible concluding prayer

Lord God, thank you that Jesus was a pioneer who did things no one else had ever done before. Sometimes the friends of Jesus doubted his power because they found it hard to trust in God. Please help us to trust in you, and help us to be good friends to others. Amen

*

The pioneer's drum: Week Four

Bible link

This week's Bible passage link is Mark 8:31–35, which recounts how Jesus told his disciples that the path he would have to take was very costly and painful, and how they didn't like what he said.

Key theme

This week's key theme is 'trust'. What makes us trust or not trust others? How important is trust in relationships? How does it feel when people trust us? How trustworthy are you? Is it important to you that people can trust you and rely on you?

It would also be possible to revisit the 'perseverance' theme. Sometimes we have to persevere at something, even when times are hard and we want to give up. Think about how it feels to stick with something and get through, and how it feels to give up and not succeed.

Episode Four

(Have the drum and drumsticks to hand.)

Do you remember our story from last time? What did this rhythm on the drum mean? *(Play the rhythm of 'Will you come and follow me?'.)* What happened when the river was struck by a storm?

Do you remember how this story about the pioneer's drum reminds us of Jesus and his disciples? They decided to follow him so that they could find out more about God.

The pioneer was still on his own, away from the camp, having a quiet rest, so all his friends crowded round to look at the map. They were very worried about what they saw. The map showed the village where they'd come from and the settlements they'd passed. It even showed the valley where the storm had hit them, but the next bit of the journey looked very dangerous indeed.

'After the next corner, there are white-water rapids,' said one of the pioneer's friends in a worried voice. 'The boat will be tipped over.' Then someone else pointed even further along the river, where the map showed a big forest. 'Giant spiders live in those trees,' he said. 'It'll be so dark, we won't be able to escape from them.' The whole group was murmuring now. 'And after the forest,' said another person, 'there are sharp underwater rocks that will wreck the boat.' He pointed at the map with a quivering hand.

'We can't go on,' said the first friend. 'After all, it's important that the pioneer can find the source of the river safely. We mustn't let him do anything dangerous.' They all agreed and started thinking of other ideas as they studied the map.

'I know!' said someone at the back of the crowd. 'We could carry the boat on a path over the land so that we don't have to go through the rapids or the forest or past the sharp rocks.' Most people thought that was a great idea, but then someone else spoke up. 'We could paddle the boat up this little stream that comes off the river,' he said as he pointed at the map. 'It goes through a gentle pool and then it joins the river again later on. We'd miss out all those dangerous things completely.' Lots of people nodded their heads as they looked carefully at the map, but then someone else started talking. 'I think it's too dangerous to try to find the source of the river. Why don't we just go back to the village now, back to our homes?'

Gradually everyone started talking and their voices got louder and louder. They began arguing over what they should do. Each of the plans sounded good and they couldn't decide which one to try. They were starting to shout at each other when suddenly they heard a noise outside the camp. *(Play the rhythm of 'Will you come and follow me?'.)* 'It's the pioneer!' they cried. They ran over to find him, all talking at once. 'We're all ready to go,' they explained, 'and the river's so dangerous that we've decided to carry the boat, or use another stream, or turn back...'

The pioneer lifted up his hands and his friends gradually stopped talking. He looked sad as he played his drum again. *(Play the rhythm of 'Will you come and follow me?'.)* 'No,' he said quietly. 'We must keep going up the river. We must risk the white-water rapids and the forest with its spiders, and even the sharp hidden rocks. That's the only way we can go.' His friends looked horrified. They started to argue with him, telling him about their other plans.

Then the pioneer began playing his drum again. *(Play the rhythm of 'Will you come and follow me?'.)* 'Will you come and follow me?' he asked. 'Will you trust me?' His friends all stood helplessly, looking at him. The pioneer played the rhythm on his drum again, the same rhythm he'd played when he first met them. *(Play the rhythm of 'Will you come and follow me?'.)* One by one they nodded their heads. 'Yes! We will trust you. We will follow you.' So they set off up the river...

I haven't got time to tell you any more of our story today. Next time we'll find out how the pioneer and his friends got on, but do you remember how this story reminds us of Jesus? He was a pioneer—someone who does things that no one else has ever done before. He shows people the way to find God.

Jesus actually said, 'Will you come and follow me?' to his disciples, but when they did follow him they soon discovered that it wasn't going to be easy. When Jesus told them what it would be like, they tried to think of another way to go. But Jesus told them to follow the 'narrow way', the hardest way, which was the only way God wanted them to go—just as the pioneer in our story told his friends that they would have to go up the most dangerous part of the river.

I wonder, would you have followed the pioneer if you'd heard his drum? *(Play the rhythm of 'Will you come and follow me?'.)* I wonder, would you have followed Jesus like the disciples did, when he called them to follow him? I wonder if you'd have trusted enough to follow Jesus, even when it wasn't easy, like the disciples did? I wonder.

Possible concluding prayer

Lord God, thank you that Jesus was a pioneer who did things no one else had ever done before. The path he took was very difficult, but he didn't try to avoid it. Please help us when things are difficult, and help us to be good friends to others. Amen

*

The pioneer's drum: Week Five

Bible link

This week's Bible passage link is Mark 10:35–45, which recounts the time when the disciples of Jesus argued about which of them was the greatest, and when Jesus told them that the greatest thing of all is to serve other people.

Key theme

This week's key theme is 'rewards'. People often do things to get rewards and praise. Jesus said that it was important to help and serve others without thinking about how you might benefit. What makes us do good things? What makes us help others? What makes us do our best work? How important are rewards, or do we do good things just because we think that's what we should do?

Episode Five

(Have the drum and drumsticks to hand.)

Do you remember our story from last time? What did this rhythm on the drum mean? *(Play the rhythm of 'Will you come and follow me?'.)* Did the pioneer's friends decide to keep on following him, even though the river looked dangerous up ahead?

Do you remember how this story about the pioneer's drum reminds us of Jesus and his disciples? They decided to follow him so that they could find out more about God.

The pioneer and his friends were back in the boat, with a drumbeat going to help them paddle smoothly. *(Play a steady drumbeat.)* As they turned the next corner, they could see that the map was correct. The water was bubbling and foaming. They were paddling into some rapids. The boat twisted and turned, but still they kept paddling *(play the drumbeat)* to a place where the water rushed through a narrow gap. The boat started tipping over, further and further. Another moment and it would completely capsize! Suddenly one of the strongest people in the boat reached out to the side and tipped the boat back again. They were safe.

Soon the rapids were behind them and they paddled on. *(Play the drumbeat.)* Up ahead they could see a big forest. Before long they were into the trees and everything was dark. Strange noises filled the air as they slid along smoothly. Suddenly they all stopped paddling. They could see a massive spider's web stretched across the river. In another moment they would be tangled up in it. The smallest person in the boat was sitting right at the front and he could see that the web was all sticky and horrible. The boat was drifting closer and closer, but then he had an idea. He grabbed a candle, lit it quickly and held it at the bottom of the web. The flames raced up and, in a few seconds, the web had completely turned to ash. They could pass safely.

Soon the forest was left behind. Still they paddled on. *(Play the drumbeat.)* They were coming to the place where sharp underwater rocks filled the river. 'I'll lean out at the front,' said one of the crew. 'I've got really good eyes and I'll watch for the rocks.' Slowly they paddled through the rocks, carefully steering past them. There were lots of wrecks everywhere. 'Left a bit!' shouted the watchman. 'Right a bit!' After ten minutes they had dodged all the rocks and were safely through.

By then, the day was almost over, so they stopped to make a camp. The pioneer said that he was going off to be quiet, on his own, and his friends all sat round the campfire talking about what had happened that day. The strong friend said, 'Do you remember how I tipped the boat back and stopped us capsizing?' Then the small friend said, 'I burnt the web so that we could get past.' 'And I watched for the rocks so we didn't get wrecked,' added the friend with really good eyes. They started arguing: 'I was the best!' 'No! I was the best!'

Then one of them noticed the pioneer's drum on the ground. 'I know!' he said. 'Why don't the three of us each play something on the drum, and the one who plays best wins!' So they took it in turns to play the most exciting rhythm they could. *(Invite three children—one big, one small, and one wearing glasses—to have a turn on the drum.)* When they'd all played the pioneer's drum, everyone started shouting out who they thought was best. *(Ask the children to vote on who they thought played the best.)*

Just then, they heard the pioneer coming back. He asked what they'd been doing with the drum, and he was very sad when they told him. 'Do you remember how we helped those ill and hungry people earlier in our journey?' he asked. 'Being the best isn't about showing off. It's about helping others and serving them, like I did before. If you want to be a real friend of mine, you must follow me and do what I do.' Then the pioneer started playing his favourite drumbeat again. *(Play the rhythm of 'Will you come and follow me?'.)* 'If you'll come and follow me, I've got an important job for you to do…' he said.

I haven't got time to tell you any more of our story today.

Next time we'll find out what that important job was, but do you remember how this story reminds us of Jesus? He was a pioneer—someone who does things that no one else has ever done before. He shows people the way to find God.

Jesus actually said, 'Will you come and follow me?' to his disciples, but when they did follow him they soon discovered that they shouldn't boast about it or show off. When two of his disciples, called James and John, asked to be the strongest and best, Jesus told them they should help and serve others instead, like he did—and they knew he was right.

I wonder, would you have followed the pioneer if you'd heard his drum? (*Play the rhythm of 'Will you come and follow me?'.*) I wonder, would you have followed Jesus like the disciples did when he called them to follow him? I wonder if you would have understood Jesus and what he said about serving others, like the disciples tried to? I wonder.

Possible concluding prayer

Lord God, thank you that Jesus was a pioneer who did things no one else had ever done before. He told his disciples how to be best by serving and helping others, not by showing off. Please help us not to show off, and help us to be good friends to others. Amen

*

The pioneer's drum: Week Six

Bible link

This week's Bible passage links are Mark 6:7–12 and 14:27–31, which recount the times when Jesus asked his disciples to go out and take his message to other people, and when he predicted that the disciples would desert him.

Key theme

This week's key theme is 'friendship and loyalty'. Think about the qualities that make a good friend. Consider how we like to do things to show our friendship and please our friends. Think about what you could do that would make one or more of your friends really happy. Think about how important it is for friends to support one another when there are problems and difficulties in life.

Episode Six

(Have the drum and drumsticks to hand.)

Do you remember our story from last time? What does this rhythm on the drum mean? *(Play the rhythm of 'Will you come and follow me?'.)* Do you remember which of the pioneer's friends was the greatest?

Do you remember how this story about the pioneer's drum reminds us of Jesus and his disciples? They decided to follow him so that they could find out more about God.

The pioneer stood looking at his friends. He had a sad face. 'I know you've come with me to try to find the source of the river, so that we can go back and tell the people in our village. But now you keep wanting to give up on our mission and find an easier journey, and you've even been arguing with each other. Are you really my friends or not?'

All his friends started talking: 'Yes! Of course we're your friends! We'd never leave you! How can you possibly doubt us? We'll stick with you, whatever happens.' But the pioneer still looked sad. 'I'm pretty sure that you'll all give up and run away from me before we get to the end of our journey,' he said, but his friends were all horrified at the idea. They said they'd definitely stay with him.

The pioneer went over to the boat to fetch the map and prepare for the next bit of the journey, but his friends all started talking together. 'How can he think we'd leave him? How can we show him that we're really his friends?' They couldn't think of anything good and soon the pioneer was back. 'I know you really want to be my friends,' he said, 'but there's something else that you must do if you want to show how strong your friendship is.' His friends were excited. 'What is it?' they asked. 'What can we do?' The pioneer held up his drum. 'You must go out into the villages near here and play them my special drumbeat. (*Play the rhythm of 'Will you come and follow me?'.*) You must ask them if they want to come and follow me as well.' The friends all looked at one another. 'Of course!' they shouted. 'That's what we must do!'

So they started practising on the drum straight away. (*Invite three children to try playing the rhythm of 'Will you come and follow me?' on the drum.*) Before long, all the pioneer's friends had learnt the rhythm and they cheered as they set off to the nearby villages. Everywhere they went, they played the pioneer's special drumbeat (*play the rhythm of 'Will you come and follow me?'*) and, most of the time, people listened. 'Come and follow the pioneer!' cried his friends wherever they played the drum (*play the rhythm of 'Will you come and follow me?'*) and sometimes new people would join them.

That evening, they all returned to the camp feeling very pleased with themselves. They'd learnt the special drumbeat and soon they would discover the source of the river. 'Just think what we'll be able to tell everyone back at our home village,' they said to one another. So they made sure the boat was all prepared, then they gathered around the pioneer. Once again he played his special rhythm. (*Play the rhythm of 'Will you come and follow me?'.*) Then he started talking in a serious voice. 'Friends,' he said, 'the river ahead is very dangerous. There is a deep ravine, completely in shadow. The sun never shines there and the water gets very, very dangerous. Are you sure you want to come with me?' He played his drum again (*play the rhythm of 'Will you come and follow me?'*) and his friends all insisted that they would stay with him.

The pioneer looked at the map and carried on talking. 'In fact, of all the many people who've tried, no one has ever survived going along this stretch of river.' His friends looked horrified. 'You mean no one at all?' they exclaimed. 'That's right,' replied the pioneer. 'No one has ever survived. Do you still want to follow me?' His friends looked at one another with shocked faces...

I haven't got time to tell you any more of our story today. It's almost finished now, so next time I'm sure we'll hear how it ends and what happened to the pioneer and his friends. Do you remember how this story reminds us of Jesus? He was a pioneer—someone who does things that no one else has ever done before. He shows people the way to find God.

Jesus actually said, 'Will you come and follow me?' to his disciples. They really wanted to show how good and strong their friendship was, even though Jesus was worried that they would all run away if the journey became too difficult for them. So when Jesus asked them to go out in pairs into the nearby villages and tell the people there all about him, that's exactly what they did. They spread the good news about Jesus and soon lots of people knew. They tried their best to be good friends.

I wonder, would you have followed the pioneer if you'd heard his drum? (*Play the rhythm of 'Will you come and follow me?'.*) Would you have tried playing his special drumbeat in the nearby villages? If Jesus had asked you, would you have set out to tell people about God, like the disciples did? I wonder.

Possible concluding prayer

Lord God, thank you that Jesus was a pioneer who did things no one else had ever done before. He asked his disciples to spread the good news about God and his love for everyone. Please help us to share the good news about you, and help us to be good friends to others. Amen

*

The pioneer's drum:
Concluding celebration

The story of 'The pioneer's drum' ends best by being connected to the beginning of Lent. One idea is to use it at an Ash Wednesday act of collective worship. The concluding episode reminds us that true friendship is very strong and can survive setbacks and even failures.

Key theme

This week's key theme is 'betrayal'. Think about how the characters in the story betrayed and abandoned the pioneer, how Judas betrayed Jesus and how the other disciples left him. How does it feel if friends let us down? How does it feel if we let down someone we care about? What makes people let others down?

Concluding episode

(Start the story by playing the rhythm of 'Will you come and follow me?' several times on the pioneer's drum.)

'The journey ahead is very dangerous! Are you really my friends or not?' That's what the pioneer said as he stepped into the boat. 'Will you come and follow me, even though no one has ever survived this bit of the river?'

It was the same with Jesus and his friends, the disciples. He asked them to follow him even though the road ahead was dangerous.

Let's get back to our story about the pioneer and his drum. Even though it was dangerous, all the pioneer's friends stayed with him—all except one. He decided that it was crazy to carry on, so he slipped away into the bushes. The pioneer and his remaining friends didn't notice he'd gone, so they got into the boat without him and started paddling on. *(Play the rhythm of 'Will you come and follow me?'.)*

The friend who'd crept away ran quickly to a nearby village. 'I need help to stop some crazy people going up the river!' he shouted. 'Quick, let's go up to the cliff-top and see what we can do!' Lots of the people from the village ran with him to the cliff. As they looked down at the river, they could see the boat. 'Hurry!' said the friend who'd run away. 'Let's roll these giant rocks over the cliff. That will block the river and they won't be able to carry on.' So they started rolling the rocks over the edge.

The pioneer and his friends were down in the deep valley, trying to paddle forward. The water was very fast and rough. The pioneer was still playing his drumbeat *(play the rhythm of 'Will you come and follow me?')* but suddenly rocks started crashing down around them from above. One landed right in front of them. Some of the friends were so terrified that they jumped out of the boat and swam to safety back down the river.

Then a whole shower of rocks came down all around them, and one smashed right through the floor of the boat. Water was rushing up through the hole and the boat was spinning round. The pioneer was still playing his drumbeat *(play the rhythm of 'Will you come and follow me?')* but then all his remaining friends gave up and jumped out of the boat. The pioneer was the only one left. The boat was sinking and more rocks were crashing down on to him from above.

The friends had all reached safety on the riverbank but, when they looked back upstream, they couldn't see the boat or the pioneer at all. They were all horrified. They'd so nearly made it to the source of the river, but now disaster had struck. 'We must search for the pioneer,' they all agreed. They searched for three days, up and down the river, but all they found were broken bits of wood. 'We weren't proper friends at all,' one of them said. 'We failed the pioneer badly.'

They decided to give up on their mission to find the source of the river, the source of life for their old village. No one would ever know about it now. Just as they were about to leave for home, though, two of the friends suddenly pointed up the river to a high place above a waterfall. They could see a man standing there in the sunshine and, as they looked, they could just hear a faint noise. (*Softly play the rhythm of 'Will you come and follow me?'.*) Suddenly they realised—*there* was the source of the river!

My story about the pioneer and his drum has come to an end now. As you know, it's a story that reminds us about Jesus. In the Bible, Jesus is called a pioneer. He goes ahead in front of us and we must keep our eyes on him if we're his friends.

Jesus said, 'Will you come and follow me?' to the disciples, and they wanted to show how good their friendship was. Although they wanted to follow Jesus all the way, they failed. One of them crept away and actually betrayed Jesus. He was called Judas and he was just like the friend in the story who threw rocks down into the river. The other disciples all ran away when things got too dangerous. Jesus was killed, just like the pioneer, who died in the river. But after three days the friends saw the pioneer up at the source of the river, the source of life, and after three days Jesus rose to new life. He still wants us to follow him and tell other people about him. That's what his disciples do.

I wonder, would you have followed the pioneer if you'd heard the drumbeat? *(Play the rhythm of 'Will you come and follow me?'.)* I wonder if you would have been like the friend who threw rocks into the river or like his other friends who all jumped out of the boat. The disciples were all like that, but they saw his true power—the true source of life from God—when Jesus rose from the dead. If you'd been one of his disciples, you would have seen it, too. And the great thing is that anyone can be a friend of Jesus. He says to everyone, 'Will you come and follow me?'

The pioneer's drum:
Ideas for classroom follow-up

RE

- Explore in more detail all the events from the life of Jesus that are paralleled in 'The pioneer's drum'.
- Starting with 'bread of life', explore the 'I am...' statements of Jesus: see www.foundationsforfreedom.net/References/NT/ Gospels/John/John00_Power-I-Am.html

English

- Read *Frederick* by Leo Lioni (Alfred A. Knopf, 1995)—a story about mice collecting provisions for winter. Frederick collects words and colours because he understands that his friends need more than just edible food to sustain them. Compare this with Jesus' claim to be the 'bread of life'.
- Read the story of the Pied Piper—a man who used an instrument to attract children to follow him. Search online for the poem by Robert Browning called 'The Pied Piper of Hamelin'.

Music

- Explore drums and drumming.

PSHE/RE/History

- Find out about organisations or charities that help sick and hungry people. Try to find out what made their founders establish these organisations and why people work for and support them today.

Geography

- Study the physical features of rivers (KS2).

General

- Research the symbolism of bread; the importance of bread around the world; staple foods in different parts of the world and the reasons for the variations.

*

Section Four

The judgment parables

Key Bible verses

'God has weighed you on his balance scales, and you fall short
of what it takes.'
DANIEL 5:27 (CEV)

Christ himself carried our sins in his body to the cross,
so that we might die to sin and live for righteousness.
It is by his wounds that you have been healed.
1 PETER 2:24

'Those who win the victory will be clothed like this in white,
and I will not remove their names from the book of the living.'
REVELATION 3:5

Values

Pride and forgiveness

This section is designed to run from after the February break until Easter. In most years the holiday begins before Easter, but sometimes the Easter weekend falls within term-time. The theme is 'The judgment parables' and, in the big story of God's love for the world, we are remembering what Jesus said about how we need to accept God's help to change, so that we can find fulfilment. When we imagine ourselves within this story, we discover what it feels like to be too proud to ask for help and what it feels like when eventually we do let someone help us.

'The chef's weighing scales' is a story told in six parts, plus a concluding episode, which illustrates some of the parables of Jesus recorded in the Bible, particularly in Matthew's Gospel.

- **Week One:** Matthew 25:1–13
- **Week Two:** Matthew 25:31–46
- **Week Three:** Matthew 22:1–14
- **Week Four:** Matthew 18:23–35
- **Week Five:** Matthew 13:24–30
- **Week Six:** Matthew 26:26–29

The storyteller's prop for 'The chef's weighing scales' consists of:

- A wooden set of balance scales made from two pieces of wood joined with a simple pivot, with two nails on which the pictures can be hung, one towards each end of the crosspiece.
- Seven pictures on card—one each of fruit cake, sponge cake, doughnut, cookie, meringue, broken loaf of bread and a 'judgment weight'. These cards should all have a small hole in them, so that they can hang on the scales, and could be laminated for durability.

Suggested music

Suggestions for pre-recorded music that could be used at the start and end of assemblies include:

- *Gloria: Sacred Choral Works* (John Rutter, Collegium B000AA4JBG)
- Mozart, Requiem (Linn B000095JS0)

Suggestions for songs that could be sung at assemblies include:

- Abba, Father, let me be
- Be still, for the presence of the Lord

- Do not be afraid
- From heaven you came, helpless babe
- God forgave my sin
- I danced in the morning
- Jesus' love is very wonderful
- There is a green hill (Week Six)

The chef's weighing scales: Week One

Bible link

This week's Bible passage link is Matthew 25:1–13, which recounts the parable of the maidens with their lamps, in which the need to make good preparations is stressed.

Key theme

This week's key theme is 'getting ready'. Sometimes it is difficult to do something properly unless we have thought carefully about it beforehand and got ourselves and other things ready. Cooking is a good example: we have to have all the right ingredients and enough of them to hand if we are to be successful. What other tasks need preparation? What happens if we don't make proper preparations? Sometimes it is important to prepare ourselves inside for things that we must do. We have to get ourselves in the right frame of mind. How might we do this?

Episode One

(Have the weighing scales and the pictures of the fruit cake and the judgment weight to hand.)

I wonder if you like cooking. Maybe you even want to become a chef?

Today I want to start a new story about a man called Gaston. All he ever wanted to do was to become a chef. He loved cooking things for other people, but he knew he needed to get his name into the Book of Chefs. To do that, he needed to go to the special Chef School.

When he got there, he was welcomed by a very important chef. 'There's only one thing you need to do,' she said. 'Look at these special weighing scales *(show the scales)*. These scales always tell the truth. All you have to do if you want to pass the test and become a chef is to bake something so light that it's lighter than the judgment weight *(show the judgment weight and put it on the scales so that they tip down)*. When you've baked something, weigh it on the scales, but remember, if it's too heavy you'll fail the test.'

Gaston decided to make his favourite fruit cake. He started with the cake mix, which he stirred together in a bowl. Next he added delicious raisins into the bowl but, while he was doing that, two other chefs came over and laughed at him. 'You mustn't add too many raisins at the start,' they said, so Gaston stopped pouring in the raisins and went and found some dried cherries. Quickly he added half the bag of cherries to the bowl, but then he remembered about his special secret ingredient— dried pineapple pieces. So in they went, too.

Just then, the two other chefs came back to see what he was doing. 'You haven't added any raisins!' they laughed. 'Look, the bag is still there on the table.' Gaston started to panic. He couldn't remember about the raisins. 'If only I'd prepared myself properly by making a list and ticking things off,' he said. 'I'll never make a good chef.' He looked over at the weighing scales with the judgment weight and wondered if he would ever pass the test.

As he stirred the mixture, Gaston noticed a man standing in the corner, holding a big brush. The man was wearing a T-shirt that said, 'If you need help, just ask me'. 'I *do* need help,' Gaston said to himself. 'Maybe I should ask that man. He looks very nice.' But as he stirred his mixture some more, Gaston thought again. 'I don't need help really,' he said proudly. 'I can do it myself. Anyway, that man is just the cleaner. He's like a servant. I don't need help from someone like him.'

Gaston tipped his mixture into the baking tin and put it into the oven. Soon it was baked and it looked delicious *(show the picture of the fruit cake)*. The moment had come for him to try to pass the test. He took his fruit cake over to the weighing scales. The judgment weight was in place *(hold up the scales and weight)*. Gaston held his breath as he put his fruit cake on the scales... *(as the fruit cake is put on the scales, ensure that it tips them down)* but it was too heavy! He'd failed the test.

A little tear came into Gaston's eye. He knew that the judgment weight and the scales always told the truth, but he really wanted to have his name written in the Book of Chefs. Then he had an idea for something else, even better, that he could cook to have another go at passing the test...

I haven't got time for any more of the story about Gaston today. Maybe next time we'll discover if he managed to bake something so light that it passed the test. But as you know, all my stories tell us something about God and Jesus. Did you know that Jesus told lots of stories about God's judgment? Just like the special weighing scales, which always tell the truth, God's judgment is always true as well.

One of the stories Jesus told about God's judgment was about ten women who went to meet someone special at night, to welcome them. It was dark and they needed lamps that burned with oil. Five of the women took spare oil and five didn't. The five who didn't take spare oil saw their lamps go out. They weren't properly prepared. They were a bit like

Gaston, who didn't manage to prepare his ingredients for the fruit cake. Gaston failed the test, just like the foolish women with no oil in their lamps, who failed their test as well.

When Jesus' friends heard this story, they asked him how they could possibly pass God's test. Jesus said, 'It's impossible for you to do it alone, but with God's help you can pass his test. You can pass his judgment, which is always true.'

I wonder what it was like for Gaston, trying to become a chef and get his name into the Book of Chefs. It must have been sad to fail with the fruit cake. I wonder what you would have tried next. And I wonder what we would have felt like if Jesus had said to us that we couldn't pass God's test unless we had his help. I wonder.

Possible concluding prayer

Lord God, you love us so much and you want us to pass your test so that we can love you too and find our names written in the Book of Life. Gaston was too proud to ask for help from the cleaner. Help us not to be like him, but make us ready to accept your help, just as Jesus said we should. Amen

*

The chef's weighing scales: Week Two

Bible link

This week's Bible passage link is Matthew 25:31–46, which recounts the parable of the sheep and the goats, stressing the need to care for our neighbour.

Key theme

This week's key theme is 'asking for help'. Sometimes it's easy to ask for help and sometimes it's difficult. What makes the difference? In Gaston's case it was about making a cake, but sometimes people have problems that are really worrying them and they find it difficult to ask for help. They keep their worries to themselves and often this just makes things worse. Explore situations around this theme, thinking about how people can be encouraged to share worries so that they can be helped.

Episode Two

(Have the weighing scales and the pictures of the sponge cake and the judgment weight to hand.)

Can you remember the story we began last time? How do these scales work? *(Show the scales with judgment weight in place.)* Who is trying to pass the test to become a chef? What did he cook last time?

Do you remember what our story reminds us about in the Bible? What did Jesus say about passing God's test?

Gaston was upset that his fruit cake was too heavy. He really wanted to get his name into the Book of Chefs, so he decided to make something much lighter. 'A sponge cake will be perfect,' he said, but then he noticed another person at the next table. She was trying to become a chef as well, but she had a broken arm in a sling. 'I can't manage to stir my mixture. Will you help me, please?' she asked Gaston, and he agreed to do his best.

She had a very sticky mixture of ingredients, with honey and a treacle sauce. It was so sticky that Gaston could hardly stir it. He realised he needed three hands—one to hold the bowl still, one to hold the recipe book open so that he could read what to do and one to stir with the wooden spoon. First of all, he tried without holding the book, but it kept shutting and he lost his place. Then he tried without holding the bowl, but it kept sliding across the table and almost on to the floor. Gaston started to get cross.

Just then, he noticed the cleaner nearby, still wearing the T-shirt that said, 'If you need help, just ask me'. 'I *do* need help,' Gaston said to himself. 'Maybe I should ask that man. He looks very nice and helpful.' But, as he looked back at the bowl and the recipe book, he remembered that this wasn't even his own cooking. 'I don't need help really,' he said proudly. 'What would the person with the broken arm think? I'm sure I can do it myself! Anyway, that man is just the cleaner. He's like a servant. I don't need help from someone like him!'

So Gaston kept on trying, but nothing worked properly. After another few minutes, he slammed the book shut angrily and stormed back to his own table. 'I'm just going to make my own!' he snapped to no one in particular, and he opened his recipe book at the page for a sponge cake. Even though he was feeling very grumpy, he soon had the ingredients mixed up in the bowl. The smell from the oven was delicious and, 30 minutes later, he held up a beautiful sponge cake, complete with thick icing in the middle and on top *(show the picture of the sponge cake)*. 'This is much better than the fruit cake,' Gaston said to himself as he carried it over to the weighing scales. The judgment weight was in place *(hold up the scales and weight)*. Gaston held his breath as he put his sponge cake on the scales… *(as the sponge cake is put on the scales, ensure that it tips them down)* but it was too heavy! He'd failed the test.

Gaston frowned. He knew that the judgment weight and the scales always told the truth, but he really wanted to have his name written in the Book of Chefs. Then he had an idea for something else, even better, that he could cook, so he could have another go at passing the test…

I haven't got time for any more of our story today. Maybe next time we'll see if Gaston managed to bake something so light that it passed the test. But I hope you remember that all my stories tell us something about God and Jesus. Did you know that Jesus told lots of stories about God's judgment? Just like the special weighing scales, which always tell the truth, God's judgment is always true as well.

One of the stories Jesus told about God's judgment was about a whole field full of sheep and goats. The shepherd separated them out so that the sheep and the goats weren't together any more. Jesus said this was a bit like what God would do with people. He said it all depended on whether people had cared properly for anyone who needed help, which is what God wants. Some people don't care for others properly—a bit like Gaston, who didn't manage to help the person with the broken arm because he was too proud to ask for help. Gaston's cake failed the test, just like the people in Jesus' story, who failed their test as well.

When Jesus' friends heard this story, they asked him how they could possibly pass God's test. Jesus said, 'It's impossible for you to do it alone, but with God's help you can pass his test. You can pass his judgment, which is always true.'

I wonder what it was like for Gaston, trying to become a chef and get his name into the Book of Chefs. Did you think his sponge cake would pass the test? What would you have tried next? And I wonder what we would have felt like if Jesus had said to us that we couldn't pass God's test unless we had his help. I wonder.

Possible concluding prayer

Lord God, you love us so much, and you want us to pass your test so that we can love you too and find our names written in the Book of Life. Gaston was too proud to ask for help from the cleaner. Help us not to be like him, but make us ready to accept your help, just as Jesus said we should. Amen

The chef's weighing scales: Week Three

Bible link

This week's Bible passage link is Matthew 22:1–14, which recounts the parable of the wedding banquet, stressing the need to accept an invitation correctly.

Key theme

This week's key theme is 'pride'. Explore positive and negative aspects of pride—for example, pride in a job well done, pride in the achievements of others and the sort of pride that is a barrier to learning or relationships.

Episode Three

(Have the weighing scales and the pictures of the doughnut and the judgment weight to hand.)

Can you remember our story from last time? What's special about these scales? *(Show the scales with judgment weight in place.)* What has Gaston tried cooking so far? Has he passed the test yet?

Do you remember what our story reminds us about in the Bible? What did Jesus say about passing God's test?

Gaston took his sponge cake off the scales. He knew the scales always told the truth, so he was very upset. He really wanted to pass the test so that he could get his name into the Book of

Chefs. 'I know!' he said. 'I'll make a doughnut!' Gaston carefully checked the ingredients. Everything looked easy except the sugar topping. He looked on all the shelves for a box of icing sugar, but he couldn't see any. He asked one of the other chefs where he could find it. 'It's in the special store room at the end of the corridor,' the chef replied. 'But you can't go there unless the head chef invites you.'

Gaston hunted for the head chef. 'Please can I get some icing sugar?' he asked. The head chef explained how anyone going into the special store room had to wear a clean chef's apron. 'If you promise to wear it, I'll invite you in,' he said. Gaston promised he would, so he went to find a clean apron. It had strings that you had to tie, and Gaston wasn't very good at knots. However much he tried to tie the apron strings behind his back, he couldn't do it.

Just then, he noticed the cleaner nearby. He was still wearing the T-shirt that said, 'If you need help, just ask me'. 'I *do* need help with these silly apron strings,' Gaston said to himself. 'Maybe I should ask that man. He looks very nice and helpful.' But, as he thought about it some more, he began to wonder if he really did need the apron anyway. 'The head chef said I could go in, after all, and I don't want to ask for help really,' he said proudly to himself. 'That man is just the cleaner. He's like a servant. I don't need help from someone like him! Anyway, this apron won't make any difference. No one will notice if I don't wear it.' So he dropped the apron on the floor.

Gaston looked around to make sure no one was watching. Quickly he ran down the corridor and into the store room, and in no time he'd grabbed the box of icing sugar. As he went back to his table, he glanced round again. No one had noticed. The sugar was perfect for the doughnut topping and, before long, Gaston had finished making it *(show the picture of the doughnut)*. 'This is perfect,' he said to himself as he carried it over to the weighing scales. The judgment weight was in place *(hold up the scales and weight)*. Gaston very carefully put his doughnut on the scales… *(as the doughnut is put on the scales, ensure that it tips them down)* but it was too heavy! He'd failed the test.

Gaston gave a cry of frustration. He knew that the judgment weight and the scales always told the truth, but he really wanted to have his name written in the Book of Chefs. Then he had another idea for something he could cook, to try to pass the test…

I haven't got time for any more of our story today. I expect next time we'll see if Gaston managed to bake something so light that it passed the test. But I hope you remember that all my stories tell us something about God and Jesus. Did you know that Jesus told lots of stories about God's judgment? Just like the special weighing scales, which always tell the truth, God's judgment is always true as well.

One of the stories Jesus told about God's judgment was about a wedding party. Lots of people were invited, but they were meant to wear proper wedding clothes. One person decided not to wear them, even though he'd been specially invited, and so he had to leave. Jesus said that this was a bit like what God would do with people. He said that God invites everyone to his party, but people must accept his invitation properly, to show they really want to be there. Some people are so proud, they decide not to accept God's invitation properly, a bit like Gaston in our story, who didn't wear the special apron because he was too proud to ask for help. Gaston's doughnut failed the test, just like the person in Jesus' story, who failed the test as well.

When Jesus' friends heard this story, they asked him how they could possibly pass God's test. Jesus said, 'It's impossible for you to do it alone, but with God's help you can pass his test. You can pass his judgment, which is always true.'

I wonder what it was like for Gaston, trying to get his name into the Book of Chefs. I wonder if you thought his doughnut would pass the test. What would you have tried next? And I wonder what we would have felt like if Jesus had said to us that we couldn't pass God's test unless we stopped being proud and accepted his help. I wonder.

Possible concluding prayer

Lord God, you love us so much, and you want us to pass your test so that we can love you too and find our names written in the Book of Life. Gaston was too proud to ask for help from the cleaner. Help us not to be like him, but make us ready to accept your help, just as Jesus said we should. Amen

The chef's weighing scales: Week Four

Bible link

This week's Bible passage link is Matthew 18:23–35, which recounts the parable of the unforgiving slave, stressing the need to forgive others as we are forgiven by God.

Key theme

This week's key theme is 'forgiveness'. Should Gaston forgive the man who tries to steal his chocolate chips? Should he share? Should we be prepared to forgive others if we want to be forgiven for things we do wrong? What makes it difficult or easy to forgive? Older children might consider who is most damaged by a failure or refusal to forgive.

Episode Four

(Have the weighing scales and the pictures of the cookie and the judgment weight to hand.)

Can you remember our story from last time? Why are these scales so important? *(Show the scales with judgment weight in place.)* What different things has Gaston tried cooking so far? Has he passed the test to become a chef yet?

Do you remember what our story reminds us about in the Bible? What did Jesus say about passing God's test?

Gaston was very upset about his doughnut, but he still really wanted to pass the test so that he could get his name written in the Book of Chefs. Then he had a brilliant idea. 'I'll make a chocolate chip cookie!' he shouted. 'That won't weigh much at all.'

It didn't take him long to find the flour and the sugar, but one thing was missing—the chocolate chips. However hard Gaston looked in all the cupboards, he couldn't find any at all. Suddenly he noticed something in the corner of the room. In among all the cleaner's brushes, down on the floor, was a big bag full of chocolate chips. The label on them said that they belonged to the cleaner. Gaston looked around, but no one seemed to be watching, so, quick as a flash, Gaston grabbed the bag and started running back to his table.

He'd only taken three steps when he crashed straight into someone. It was the cleaner! 'What are you doing?' asked the cleaner. Gaston was shaking with fear but he decided to be honest. 'I'm very sorry,' he said. 'I need some chocolate chips, and I know it's very bad, but I took your bag. Please forgive me.' The cleaner smiled at him. 'I forgive you. You can have my bag if you want.'

Gaston was delighted. He poured out a pile of chocolate chips on his table and went to wash his hands, ready to mix them in. Just as he was coming back to his place, he saw something that made him very angry. One of the other chefs was stealing from his pile of chocolate chips. Gaston sprinted over and grabbed the thief. 'What are you doing?' he screamed angrily. 'That's my pile of chocolate chips. Hands off!' The other chef was shaking with fear. 'I'm very sorry, Gaston,' he said, 'but I really need some of these chocolate chips for my recipe. I know it's bad, but I thought I could take some of yours. Please forgive me.' Gaston was furious. 'You're a thief!' he yelled. 'You should be put in prison! I certainly won't forgive you and you can't have any of my chocolate chips!' Then he pushed the other chef away empty-handed. He was very proud to have stopped such a naughty thief, but the cleaner, who was watching from his corner, was filled with sadness.

Gaston finished making his cookie *(show the picture of the cookie)*. Then he took it over to the weighing scales. The judgment weight was in place *(hold up the scales and weight)*. He very carefully put his cookie on the scales... *(as the cookie is put on the scales, ensure that it tips them down)* but it was too heavy! He'd failed the test.

Gaston was full of despair. He knew that the judgment weight and the scales always told the truth, but he really wanted to have his name written in the Book of Chefs. 'Maybe I should give up,' he said to himself. But then he had one last idea...

I haven't got time for any more of our story today. I expect next time we'll see if Gaston's final idea passed the test. I hope you remember that all my stories tell us something about God and Jesus. Did you know that Jesus told lots of stories about God's judgment? Just like the special weighing scales, which always tell the truth, God's judgment is always true as well.

One of the stories Jesus told about God's judgment was about someone who didn't forgive. It was a person who'd taken a fortune from the king, but the king let him off completely. Later on, the person who'd been forgiven met one of his friends who owed him a small amount of money, but he wouldn't let him off. He even had him put in prison. Jesus explained that God forgives us for so much, just like the king, and we make a mistake if we don't forgive each other—a bit like Gaston in our story, who didn't forgive the other chef even though the cleaner had forgiven him. Gaston's cookie failed the test, just like the person in Jesus' story, who failed the test as well.

When Jesus' friends heard this story, they asked him how they could possibly pass God's test. Jesus said, 'It's impossible for you to do it alone, but with God's help you can pass his test. You can pass his judgment, which is always true.'

If you'd been Gaston, I wonder how you'd have felt when the cleaner found you taking his bag of chocolate chips. And what would you have done when someone else tried stealing from your pile? Would you have been too proud to forgive them? I wonder what we would have felt like if Jesus had said to us that we couldn't pass God's test unless we stopped being proud and accepted his help. I wonder.

Possible concluding prayer

Lord God, you love us so much, and you want us to pass your test so that we can love you too and find our names written in the Book of Life. Gaston was too proud to ask for help from the cleaner. Help us not to be like him, but make us ready to accept your help, just like Jesus said we should. Amen

The chef's weighing scales: Week Five

Bible link

This week's Bible passage link is Matthew 13:24–30, which recounts the parable of the weeds in the field, stressing the need to be patient and allow God alone to sort out good from evil.

Key theme

This week's key theme is 'prejudice and social divisions'. Some people think that others are less important than they are. They believe they are better than others. This leads to feelings of prejudice and unfair judgment. What does Gaston the chef really know about the cleaner? Is he right to think he is better than him? How might things be different if he didn't have these feelings? What do you think is going to happen between them in the next part of the story?

Episode Five

(Have the weighing scales and the pictures of the meringue and the judgment weight to hand.)

Can you remember the story we're hearing? What do these scales do? *(Show the scales with judgment weight in place.)* What different things has Gaston tried cooking so far? Has he got his name written in the Book of Chefs yet?

And do you remember what our story reminds us about in the Bible? What did Jesus say about passing God's test?

Gaston couldn't understand why the things he'd cooked had all failed the test on the scales. If only he could think of something really light. He looked through the recipe book one last time, and then he saw a picture of a meringue. 'Of course!' he said with delight. 'A meringue is the lightest thing you can possibly cook. I must make a meringue.'

Gaston checked the recipe and discovered that he needed some eggs, because meringues are made from egg whites. Luckily there was a box of eggs in the store cupboard, so he started cracking them into a glass bowl. But every time he cracked an egg open and poured the egg white in, some of the shell seemed to go in as well. Soon it was quite a mess. Gaston fetched a spoon and started trying to scoop the pieces of shell out. It took ages and he was feeling very impatient and cross. 'These stupid shells,' he said grumpily. 'Why did they have to break into the bowl? Why can't I get them out?'

Just then, Gaston noticed the cleaner nearby. He was still wearing the T-shirt that said, 'If you need help, just ask me'. 'I *do* need help with these stupid pieces of shell,' he mumbled to himself. 'Maybe I should ask the cleaner. He looks as though he would help me.' But then he realised how silly he'd been to get bits of shell into the bowl in the first place. 'I can't ask the cleaner to help,' he said to himself proudly. 'He's just a servant. I don't need help from someone like him! If I can't get the shell out myself, I'm sure no one will notice.' So he scraped his spoon impatiently around the bowl a few more times and gave up trying.

Instead, he added some sugar and got an electric whisk out of the drawer. In no time at all, he had a bowl full of airy light mixture, which made lots of small meringues. After they had been in the oven, they were even lighter, and Gaston chose the lightest meringue of all *(show the picture of the meringue)*. Then he took it over to the weighing scales, proudly holding it up high so that all the other chefs could see it. A crowd gathered round as Gaston reached the scales. The judgment weight was in place *(hold up the scales and weight)*. 'At last,' he was thinking. 'Soon I will get my name written in the Book of Chefs.' He very carefully put his meringue on the scales… *(as the meringue is put on the scales, ensure that it tips them down)* but it was too heavy! He'd failed the test again.

Gaston couldn't believe it. The meringue was almost lighter than air. How could it have failed the test? He knew that the judgment weight and the scales always told the truth. Slowly he turned away with tears in his eyes. He'd never be a chef now. He pushed his way past the crowd, but suddenly someone was in his way, not letting him past. It was the cleaner. On his T-shirt Gaston could read, 'If you need help, just ask me'. Gaston stopped. Then he opened his mouth to say something…

I haven't got time for any more of our story today. Maybe next time we'll discover what Gaston wanted to say. But I hope you remember that all my stories tell us something about God and Jesus. Did you know that Jesus told lots of stories about God's judgment? Just like the special weighing scales, which always tell the truth, God's judgment is always true as well.

One of the stories Jesus told about God's judgment was about a field full of good wheat and nasty weeds, all mixed up. The farmer had to wait patiently until harvest time before they could be separated, good from bad. Jesus explained that it's the same with God. Everyone is a mixture of good and bad, and we must wait patiently for God to help take the bad bits away. If we're impatient and proud, we'll forget to ask for help. Gaston, in our story, was impatient. He wouldn't ask for help so he failed the test with his meringue.

When Jesus' friends heard this story, they asked him how they could possibly pass God's test. Jesus said, 'It's impossible for you to do it alone, but with God's help you can pass his test. You can pass his judgment, which is always true.'

I wonder what it felt like for Gaston when even his meringue failed the test. If you'd been him, wouldn't you have been very sad not to get your name into the Book of Chefs? And I wonder what we would have felt like if Jesus had said to us that we couldn't pass God's test unless we stopped being proud and accepted his help. I wonder.

Possible concluding prayer

Lord God, you love us so much, and you want us to pass your test so that we can love you too and find our names written in the Book of Life. Gaston was too proud to ask for help from the cleaner. Help us not to be like him, but make us ready to accept your help, just as Jesus said we should. Amen

The chef's weighing scales: Week Six

Bible link

This week's Bible passage link is Matthew 26:26–29, which recounts the time when Jesus shared bread and wine at the last supper and explained that he was giving his life to take away the mistakes made by human beings.

Key theme

This week's key theme is 'judgment'. Judgment is something that happens a lot in school. Just as Gaston's cooking was judged, so our work is judged, but not for quite the same reasons. Explore the reasons why teachers mark work and say what is good about it and what could be better. It's all about identifying and aiming for goals.

Episode Six

(Have the weighing scales and the pictures of the broken bread and the judgment weight to hand.)

Can you remember what's happened in our story? What did Gaston weigh on the scales? *(Show the scales with judgment weight in place.)* Do you think he should make something else to try to pass the test? What could he do to make a difference?

Do you remember what our story reminds us about in the Bible? What did Jesus say about passing God's test?

Gaston was feeling very upset. Why couldn't he be a chef? Why did he keep failing the test with the scales and the judgment weight? As he stood in front of the cleaner, he started telling him how sad he was. Then he noticed the words on the cleaner's T-shirt again: 'If you need help, just ask me'. 'He's only the cleaner!' said Gaston to himself. 'He's only a servant! He can't help me.' But something about the cleaner's kind face made Gaston ask, 'Have you got an idea for something I could cook?'

The cleaner smiled and asked Gaston what he'd tried already. 'Well, I started with a fruit cake,' replied Gaston. 'Then I made a sponge cake, then a doughnut, then a cookie. Last of all, I made a meringue, but none of them passed the test.' 'I've got an idea,' said the cleaner. 'Let's go and look in the store cupboard.' Gaston followed the cleaner and they found a bag of flour.

'All we need to do is add some yeast and a bit of water,' said the cleaner, and that's just what they did. Soon they had a small lump of plain dough, ready to be baked. It made a lovely smell as it rose in the oven and, at just the right moment, the cleaner took it out so that it could cool down.

Gaston looked at the tiny loaf of bread. He wasn't sure if it looked lighter than any of the other things he'd made. The cleaner picked it up. 'Feel how light it is!' he said. 'And look, if I break the bread, you'll see how good it is.' The cleaner broke the bread and Gaston saw how beautiful it was *(show the picture of the broken bread)*. Then the cleaner said, 'Why not try weighing this bread on the weighing scales? Maybe it will pass the test.'

Gaston carefully took the bread over to the scales. He was about to start weighing it to see if it was lighter than the judgment weight when the cleaner stopped him. 'Do you know you can turn the scales the other way up?' he said with a smile. 'They work best when you turn them upside down.' So Gaston turned the scales the other way up *(turn the scales so that they look like a cross, still with the judgment weight in place)*. He could see that they looked just like a cross. Everything had gone completely quiet in the whole kitchen. People were watching as Gaston carefully lifted up the broken bread. He paused for a moment. Then he put the bread on the scales... *(as the bread is put on the scales, ensure that the scales stay up)*. It was so light, it passed the test. Gaston felt all his sadness disappear. He could forget about all the times he'd failed. He gave a great shout of joy!

Our story has almost finished now: there's just one last bit for next time. I'm sure you remember that this story tells us something very special about God and how he loves us. Jesus told lots of stories about God's judgment, and he explained how nobody can pass God's test on their own without help.

I wonder if you've worked out who the cleaner reminds us of. The cleaner was just a servant but he cared for Gaston and wanted to help him. In fact, the cleaner reminds us of Jesus, who is sometimes called the Servant-King. The cleaner's T-shirt said, 'If you need help, just ask me', and that's exactly what Jesus says to everyone: 'If you need help, just ask me.'

On the night before Jesus was betrayed and captured by his enemies, he had a meal with his friends. He took some bread, broke it and said, 'This is my body given for you—it takes away your failings.' Then he did the same with a cup of wine. The very next day, Jesus died on the cross. When he did that, he took away everything we've ever done wrong. He showed people how much God loves them.

Our story about Gaston and the cleaner reminds us of what Jesus did. Gaston only passed the test when the weighing scales became a cross and when the bread that the cleaner had broken was weighed on the scales. Gaston couldn't pass the test himself—he needed the cleaner's help—and we can only pass God's judgment if Jesus helps us. He is a Servant-King.

If you'd been Gaston, would you have asked the cleaner for help, even though he was just a servant? How would you have felt when the broken bread passed the test? I wonder if you'd have shouted for joy. And I wonder if we will really accept Jesus' help when we need it, so that we can pass God's judgment. I wonder.

Possible concluding prayer

Lord God, you love us so much, and you want us to pass your test so that we can love you too and find our names written in the Book of Life. In the end, Gaston asked for help from the cleaner. Help us to be like him, and make us ready to accept your help, just as Jesus said we should. Amen

The chef's weighing scales: Concluding celebration

The story of 'The chef's weighing scales' ends with a Holy Week or Easter celebration. The concluding episode reminds us that Christians believe that Jesus gave us life because of what he did at Easter.

Key theme

This week's key theme is 'happiness'. What is complete happiness? The story says that we are truly happy when we become the kind of people God wants us to be. What do you think that means? Do you agree? What would make you completely happy?

Concluding episode

(Have the weighing scales and all six pictures to hand.)

Do you remember Gaston? He went to Chef School to learn how to become a proper chef, but he had to pass the test before he could have his name added to the Book of Chefs. He had to cook something that was so light, it wouldn't tip the scales with the judgment weight. He tried making lots of different things, but they all failed the test. In the end, the cleaner, who was just a servant, helped him make some bread and showed him how to turn the scales upside down so that they looked like a cross *(show the scales with the judgment weight and the broken bread)*. At last Gaston had passed the test.

Gaston looked up at the weighing scales and thought about what had happened. 'Now I can see why I didn't pass the test earlier,' he said. 'I was too proud. I didn't want to ask for help when I needed it. I thought I could pass the test on my own. Each time things went wrong, I noticed the cleaner there, wearing his T-shirt that said, "If you need help, just ask me", but my pride stopped me asking and I made mistakes. Then, at last, I let the cleaner help me. All my mistakes were forgotten and I passed the test.'

Gaston could see the cleaner standing nearby. He was still wearing his special T-shirt saying, 'If you need help, just ask me', and he had a big smile on his face. Gaston went over to say 'thank you' to the cleaner, but he wanted to ask about all the things he'd made before. 'I feel very silly that I made all those other things,' he said to the cleaner. 'The fruit cake, the sponge cake, the doughnut, the cookie and the meringue (*show each picture in turn*). I don't know why I bothered.' But the cleaner said, 'None of them was wasted. It was good that you made them all, because you learnt how hard it is to pass the test. If it was easy, it wouldn't be special.'

Just then, a very important-looking person came into the kitchen and everyone went quiet. He started talking. 'You all know that these weighing scales and the judgment weight always tell the truth. When the weight stays down, the test has been passed, and someone has just passed the test—Gaston!' Everyone cheered and clapped. Gaston laughed with delight and the cleaner did, too. The important person carried on talking. 'When someone passes the test, they get their name written in the Book of Chefs.' He pulled out a great big book, opened it and, using a quill pen, he wrote Gaston's name in the book. Gaston was so excited. At last he would be completely happy. He could do the thing he'd always wanted to do.

Now, this story about Gaston and the weighing scales is a very special story because it tells us something about God and about Jesus. You'll remember, I'm sure, that Jesus told lots of stories, called parables, about God's judgment. Just like the special weighing scales and the judgment weight in our story, which always told the truth, God's judgment is always true as well.

When Jesus' friends asked him how they could possibly pass God's test, he said, 'It's impossible for you to do it alone, but with God's help you can pass his test. You can pass his judgment, which is always true.' In fact, it is only because of Jesus our Servant-King, who broke the bread at the last supper to take away our failures and died on the cross to take away the burden of our sins, that we pass God's judgment. God forgives us for anything, so long as we let Jesus help us. It's a bit like in our story, when the cleaner helped Gaston to pass the test at Chef School by making and breaking bread for him and by turning the scales into a cross. It says in the Bible that everyone who wins the victory will have their name in 'the book of the living'.

Gaston was so pleased when his name was actually written into the Book of Chefs by the very important person. He laughed with delight. He knew he'd be completely happy. That's what it feels like when someone knows that their name is in the Book of Life. They know it's only because of Jesus and what he did at Easter time, when he died on a cross and rose again on the third day. They know that when their name is in the Book of Life, they will be completely happy because they'll become just like God wants them to be. When we ask Jesus for help, it can be true for us as well.

I wonder what it was like for Gaston, becoming a proper chef and getting his name into the Book of Chefs. Can you imagine being like him? It must have been very special to receive that help from the cleaner. Every time someone asks Jesus for help and gets their name written in the Book of Life, that's very special indeed. It's the most special thing in the whole world, and it's what we celebrate at Easter time.

*

The chef's weighing scales: Ideas for classroom follow-up

RE

- Read and explore the parables paralleled in the story of the chef's weighing scales. Discuss the lessons in them. Think about their application and relevance to pupils' lives and their understanding of life.
- Link the parable of the unforgiving servant with the line in the Lord's Prayer that says, 'Forgive us our sins as we forgive those who sin against us.' Consider the Jewish tradition that if a person is genuinely sorry and asks forgiveness of a person they've wronged, and has to ask three times, continually having their request rejected, then the sin passes across to the person who was sinned against.

English

- Use some of the stories to fulfil requirements of the English curriculum.

Design Technology

- Devise and make the best cake ever.

*

Section Five

The first Christians

Key Bible verse

All of you are Christ's body, and each one is a part of it.
1 CORINTHIANS 12:27

Values

Happiness and unity

This section is designed to run from after Easter until the late May break. The theme is 'The first Christians' and, in the big story of God's love for the world, we are remembering the time when he encouraged and unified the members of the early church. When we imagine ourselves within this part of the story, we discover what it feels like to be facing great challenges and overcome them, and we find out the importance of every separate person in a community.

'Pavlov's power-suit' is a story told in six parts, plus a concluding episode, which illustrates the biblical account of how the first Christians received the power of the Holy Spirit and the things they did. It is found in the book of Acts.

- Week One: Acts 2:1–4
- Week Two: Acts 2:42–47
- Week Three: Acts 3:1–10
- Week Four: Acts 8:26–35
- Week Five: Acts 10:34–43
- Week Six: Acts 13:1–3

The storyteller's prop used for 'Pavlov's power-suit' consists of six separate items of clothing that make up the 'suit':

- Two leg-protectors, made of shin guards
- Two arm-protectors, made of shin guards (the straps may need shortening)
- A hat
- A glove

Each item in the power-suit could be in a different bright colour.

Each item of the suit has an electric socket (simple extension lead) fixed to it, with a 2-metre length of thin flex attached and an electric plug on the end. These are designed so that each part of the suit can be connected to another part. The glove should have a simple battery-operated 'push' light stuck on it. The sockets can be attached to the items of clothing by stitching or taping them in place.

Suggested music

Suggestions for pre-recorded music that could be used at the start and end of assemblies include:

- Theme music from *Superman* or *Star Wars* (*The Greatest Movie Themes*, Music Digital B001EGKYZ0)
- *The Lark Ascending* (Vaughan Williams, Double Decca B000000IX81)

Suggestions for songs that could be sung at assemblies include:

- A new commandment
- All over the world

- Bind us together, Lord
- Lord, the light of your love is shining
- The Spirit lives to set us free

*

Pavlov's power-suit: Week One

Bible link

This week's Bible passage link is Acts 2:1–4, which recounts the day of Pentecost, when the apostles received the Holy Spirit and could speak in many languages.

Key theme

This week's key theme is 'communication'. Consider how important and helpful it is to be able to communicate with others in ways that they understand, speaking their language. This might mean literally a foreign language or a different dialect or style of speech, or it might mean responding in ways that meet the needs of particular emotional situations, to bring comfort. Another theme is 'inspiration'. The disciples received the Holy Spirit to comfort, inspire and energise them. Who or what inspires us?

Episode One

(Have the six parts of the power-suit to hand.)

I wonder if you've ever invented anything really clever. Well, today I'd like to start telling a story about a man who was an inventor. His name was Pavlov. He loved inventing new things. Once he invented a special kind of bread that always fell butter side up. Another time, he invented some special glasses that meant you could watch TV and play a computer game all at once.

One day, Pavlov got a letter. The letter explained about a

really difficult challenge—to invent something that would help a person survive for a whole week on the most dangerous mountain in the world. Pavlov started thinking. He wondered about a special tent for camping in. Another idea he had was to make an everlasting hot-water bottle. In the end, though, he decided to invent a power-suit, which would help him survive when he wore it. The power-suit had six parts—a hat, two arm protectors, two leg protectors, and a glove. *(Show the children the bits of the power-suit and ask for a volunteer to wear it. 'Dress' the volunteer. At this stage, the different parts are still connected only to themselves.)*

The suit was a perfect fit and Pavlov was very pleased. 'The mountain is very dangerous, but I'm sure I'll survive with this suit on,' he thought to himself. So he set off on to the mountain. It was very windy and cold. In fact, it was the worst weather there had ever been on the mountain. The wind howled around him and kept blowing him over. It got colder and colder and he started to shiver. Then it started snowing and he was getting completely buried.

Pavlov started pleading with the weather. 'Please change!' he said, but things just got worse. He was very frightened, but then he remembered about the power-suit. Now, the special thing about Pavlov's power-suit was this. You could connect up all the different parts, using wires. When it was connected properly, the light on the glove would turn on. Then the suit's amazing powers would begin to work. Pavlov didn't quite know what those powers were, but he was hoping they would help him survive on the mountain. *(Move the electric plugs to differently coloured sockets so that every part of the suit is connected together. Switch the light on as the last connection is made.)*

Suddenly the light on the glove came on. Pavlov could feel the suit fill with power. He started talking to the weather again. He said to the wind, 'Please stop blowing, wind!' His voice sounded strange, as if it was speaking a special 'wind' language so that the wind could hear it. And it stopped blowing! Then Pavlov said to the snow, 'Please stop falling, snow!' His voice sounded different again, more like a special 'snow' language. And the snow stopped falling! In fact, Pavlov found that the suit had given him power to speak to all the different kinds of weather and they all listened to him. Before long, the first day had come to an end and Pavlov was delighted that he had survived. 'Without the power-suit, I wouldn't have managed,' he said to himself. He settled down to sleep for the night and wondered what dangerous things would happen the next day…

I haven't got time for any more of our story today. We'll find out some more about what happened to Pavlov next time. This story reminds us about God and things in the Bible. We've just had the Easter holiday, and Easter is the time when we remember that Jesus rose to life again. But although the friends of Jesus were excited about what had happened, they felt very frightened as well. Everyone around them seemed to be against them. The world was a very dangerous place, just like the mountain that Pavlov was on. Those friends of Jesus were the very first Christians and they wondered how they could survive, but God sent them some very special help.

One day, the first Christians were all together in a room when the Holy Spirit appeared on them like flames of fire. It gave them the power to do amazing things, and the first thing they could do was to speak in many different languages. It was just like Pavlov's power-suit, which gave him the power to speak in different languages to the weather. The Christians used their new power to explain about Jesus to all the different people nearby.

The Bible explains what it felt like. The first Christians couldn't do anything on their own. They had to be like a 'body' together, just like Pavlov's power-suit with its different bits. The power only worked when it was all joined up, and the first Christians were just the same. They were all joined together by God. No one was missing. When everyone was joined together, they felt an amazing power working among them.

I wonder what it was like to be Pavlov and to go on to the dangerous mountain wearing his suit. It must have been amazing when the light came on and the suit started working! And I wonder what it was like, being one of those first Christians, living in a dangerous world. It must have been amazing to be all joined up like a body with the others and to feel God's power working. I wonder what it was really like. I wonder.

Possible concluding prayer

Lord God, the first Christians faced lots of dangers but you kept them joined together and you sent a new kind of power to help them—a power that meant they could speak many languages. Help us to be joined together with each other so that we can feel your power with us, too. Amen

Pavlov's power-suit: Week Two

Bible link

This week's Bible passage link is Acts 2:42–47, which recounts the time when the first Christians shared everything together.

Key theme

This week's key theme is 'sharing and working together'. Consider the benefits of sharing and working together in a variety of situations. Talk about how sharing and working together made a difference on the mountain. Another theme is 'learning lessons'. Pavlov might have used the power-suit to help him make a fire but, instead, he used it to persuade the three friends to share what they already had. Think about how this principle is applied in helping the world's starving people, not just providing food but also providing training and equipment that enables them to produce food for themselves.

Episode Two

(Have the six parts of the power-suit to hand, ensuring that they are separate.)

Do you remember our story from last time? What was the name of the inventor? And what challenge did he face? Do you remember how the power-suit worked? *('Dress' a volunteer in the suit. At this stage, the different parts are still connected only to themselves.)* Do you remember how this story reminds us of the first Christians and how, when they were all joined up together, an amazing power was given to them?

Pavlov was pleased that he'd survived the first day on the mountain, but he could feel his fingers getting frozen and his nose had icicles hanging from it. Dark clouds came sweeping over the mountain and hailstones started falling out of the sky. Soon Pavlov was shivering and his teeth were chattering. 'I've never been so cold in my life!' he thought to himself. 'How can I keep warm?'

Pavlov stumbled round the edge of a giant rock and was surprised to see three other people sheltering from the hailstones. To start with, he thought they were frozen solid. They were sitting against the rock and their eyes were shut, but then he noticed they were breathing, so he shouted above the noise of the wind and asked them how long they'd been there. 'This is the second day we've been stuck behind this rock,' said one of them. 'We're freezing to death now,' added another. 'If only we could warm ourselves up,' said the third.

Pavlov could see that they had rucksacks. 'Haven't you got something to make a fire with?' he asked them, but the wind was blowing so hard that they couldn't hear him. So Pavlov sat down next to the first person and shouted in their ear. 'Well, I've got some wood,' replied the person, 'but I haven't got anything to light it with.' Then Pavlov crouched next to the second person. 'I have got a box of matches,' answered the second person, 'but that's no good on its own.' When Pavlov asked the third person what they had in their rucksack, he was shown a can of special fire-lighting fluid. But none of the three people wanted to show the others what they had. 'It's my store of emergency supplies,' each one said. 'I might need it.' However hard Pavlov tried to explain about making a fire, none of them would listen.

Then Pavlov remembered the power-suit he was wearing. 'Maybe the suit's powers will help me,' he said to himself, so he started joining the connections. *(Move the electric plugs to different-coloured sockets so that every part of the suit is connected together. Switch the light on as the last connection is made.)* Suddenly the light on the glove came on. Pavlov could feel the suit filling with power. He opened his mouth and his voice seemed much more powerful now. 'Friends, share your wood and your matches and your fire-lighting fluid!' he boomed. 'Don't keep them hidden for yourselves! Share them, and you'll survive.'

The three people were listening to him now, and soon they'd shared their wood and matches and fire-lighting fluid, and a blazing fire was keeping them warm. They started chatting and laughing. Pavlov laughed as well. 'Without the power-suit, I wouldn't have managed,' he smiled to himself. Then, with a wave to his three new friends, he set off along the path again, wondering what dangerous things would happen next...

I haven't got time for any more of our story today. We'll find out some more about what happened to Pavlov next time. Do you remember how this story reminds us about God and things in the Bible? The first Christians lived in a very dangerous world, just like the dangerous mountain that Pavlov was on. Those friends of Jesus wondered how they could survive, but God sent them some very special help.

People normally like to keep their own things safe for themselves, and the first Christians started out just the same. They were like the three frozen people on the mountain, but God sent the Holy Spirit and it gave them the power to do amazing things. It helped them share everything they had with each other, even their homes. It was just like Pavlov's power-suit, which gave him the power to help the people on the mountain share their things. The Christians used that power to show how God wants us to share everything we have.

The Bible explains what it felt like. The first Christians couldn't do anything on their own. They had to be like a 'body' together, just like Pavlov's power-suit with its different bits. The power only worked when it was all joined up, and the first Christians were just the same. They were all joined together by God. No one was missing. When everyone was joined together, they felt an amazing power working among them.

I wonder what it was like to be Pavlov on that freezing mountain. It must have been amazing when the light came on and the suit started working. And I wonder what it was like being one of those first Christians, living in a dangerous world. It must have been amazing to be all joined up like a body with the others and to feel God's power working. I wonder what it was really like. I wonder.

Possible concluding prayer

Lord God, the first Christians faced lots of dangers, but you kept them joined together and you sent a new kind of power to help them—a power that meant they could share everything they had. Help us to be joined together with each other so that we can feel your power with us, too. Amen

Pavlov's power-suit: Week Three

Bible link

This week's Bible passage link is Acts 3:1–10, which recounts the time when Peter healed a beggar instead of giving him money.

Key theme

This week's key theme is 'miracles'. Pavlov managed to help the man on the mountain and Peter managed to heal the beggar. These were amazing happenings. What do pupils think about miracles? In what different ways do we use the word 'miracle'? Consider what people mean by terms like 'miracles of nature', 'miracles of medicine', 'miracles of science' and so on. Do we think that the man on the mountain was physically healed or was he encouraged to find the inner strength to get down the mountain?

Episode Three

(Have the six parts of the power-suit to hand, ensuring that they are separate.)

Do you remember our story from last time? Do you remember how the power-suit worked? *('Dress' a volunteer in the suit. At this stage, the different parts are still connected only to themselves.)*

Do you remember how this story reminds us of the first Christians and how, when they were all joined up together, an amazing power was given to them?

Pavlov kept walking up the mountain, even though the wind was howling around him. He could see a place where he would be able to shelter, so he pressed on through the snow. Suddenly he stumbled over something on the ground. He thought it might be a rock, but it felt too soft for that. Then he noticed with surprise that whatever it was seemed to be moving. It was a man who'd been badly injured. 'Please help me!' said the man to Pavlov with a weak voice, so Pavlov tried to think what he could do.

The man had a big bruise on his head, and Pavlov thought it needed a bandage, but, after looking in his rucksack, he realised he didn't have any bandages. As Pavlov looked at the man a bit more closely, he could see blood coming from a cut on one of his hands. 'That needs a plaster,' said Pavlov with a worried voice, but he didn't even have any plasters in his rucksack. The man was still lying on the ground, groaning in pain. 'You need some painkillers,' thought Pavlov to himself. 'Maybe I've got some of that special bright-coloured medicine that helps stop the pain.' But he couldn't find any at all.

By now, Pavlov was getting very worried. He didn't think there was anything he could do to help the injured man, but then he thought of his power-suit. Perhaps, if he connected it up, it would help him. (*Move the electric plugs to different-coloured sockets so that every part of the suit is connected together. Switch the light on as the last connection is made.*) Suddenly the light on the glove came on! Pavlov could feel the suit filling with power. He opened his mouth and started talking to the man with a powerful voice. 'I haven't got any bandages or plasters or painkillers, but whenever I connect up this suit and the light comes on, I find I can do amazing things. I command you now to stand up and walk!'

As he spoke, Pavlov could hardly believe his eyes. The man started getting to his feet. He could walk again, and off he went down the mountain with a big smile on his face. Pavlov was smiling too, and the light on his power-suit was still shining. 'This suit really has got amazing powers when I connect it all up,' he said to himself as he reached the place where he could shelter. That day was almost over but Pavlov realised that he still had a long way to go before he'd survived a whole week. And as he looked out of his shelter, he saw something that filled his heart with dread...

There's no time for any more of our story today, but we'll find out some more about what happened to Pavlov next time. Do you remember how this story reminds us about God and things in the Bible? The first Christians lived in a very dangerous world, just like the dangerous mountain Pavlov was on. Those friends of Jesus wondered how they could survive, but God sent them some very special help.

I wonder if you remember one of the first Christians, called Peter. One day, Peter met a poor beggar who was crippled and very ill, just like the injured man who Pavlov met on the mountain. The man asked Pavlov to help him and the beggar pleaded for help from Peter. Peter didn't have any money to give the beggar, and Pavlov was just the same. He didn't have any bandages or plasters or painkillers, but when he connected up his power-suit it gave him an amazing power to help the injured man. That's just what happened with Peter and the beggar. Peter said, 'In the name of Jesus, get up and walk' and the power of the Holy Spirit made it happen.

The Bible explains what it felt like. The first Christians couldn't do anything on their own. They had to be like a 'body' together, just like Pavlov's power-suit with its different bits. The power-suit only worked when it was all joined up, and the first Christians were just the same. They were all joined together by God. No one was missing. When everyone was joined together, they felt an amazing power working among them.

I wonder what it was like to be Pavlov on that freezing mountain. Would you have stopped to help the injured man? It must have been amazing when the light came on and the suit started working. And I wonder what it was like being one of those first Christians, living in a dangerous world. I wonder what it was like for Peter when he met the beggar. It must have been amazing to be all joined up like a body with the others, and to feel God's power working. I wonder what it was really like. I wonder.

Possible concluding prayer

Lord God, the first Christians faced lots of dangers, but you kept them joined together and you sent a new kind of power to help them—a power that meant they could heal people who were in need. Help us to be joined together with each other so that we can feel your power with us too. Amen

Pavlov's power-suit: Week Four

Bible link

This week's Bible passage link is Acts 8:26–35, which recounts the time when Philip explained about Jesus to the Ethiopian.

Key theme

This week's key theme is 'guidance'. Think of different situations in which we do not fully understand or times when we do not quite know what to do for the best, which way to turn or how to resolve a difficulty. To whom or to what might we turn in these different situations, to help us understand and work things out? How does learning in school help us with our understanding of life? How is it like the map that Pavlov looked at on the mountain?

Episode Four

(Have the six parts of the power-suit to hand, ensuring that they are separate.)

Do you remember our story from last time? Do you remember how the power-suit worked? *('Dress' a volunteer in the suit. At this stage, the different parts are still connected only to themselves.)*

Do you remember how this story reminds us of the first Christians and how, when they were all joined up together, an amazing power was given to them?

Pavlov had found a good place to shelter on the mountain, but, as he looked out across the valley, he became very frightened.

He could see a great big snowstorm rushing in from the east, so he decided to try to get round the side of the mountain for protection. He struggled through the thick blanket of snow, but it was almost impossible to move.

In the end, Pavlov managed to drag himself round the corner of a rock. He was very surprised to see a man sitting there with a map. The man was surprised to see Pavlov as well, but he soon explained that he was lost and he couldn't read his map. Pavlov looked at the map but it didn't seem to make any sense. He scratched his head and tried to think what the lines and writing could mean. 'How can I work it out?' he said to himself. Then Pavlov thought of his power-suit. 'Maybe, if I connect it up, it will help me to understand this puzzling map,' he thought. *(Move the electric plugs to different-coloured sockets so that every part of the suit is connected together. Switch the light on as the last connection is made.)*

Suddenly the light on the glove came on! Pavlov could feel the suit filling with power. He took the map from the man and looked carefully at it again. This time it all began to make sense. He could see what the lines meant. Some of them marked contour lines, to show the height above sea level. Where the mountainside was very steep, the lines were close together. Other lines marked all the pathways on the mountain and even tunnels. 'No wonder it was hard to understand at first,' said Pavlov to the man, 'but now I can see everything.'

'Look!' said Pavlov. 'This is where we are, and this path leads further round the mountain. There should be a tunnel here, which will take you up to a safe valley.' The man was delighted. 'What is that suit you're wearing?' he asked. 'It seems to be very powerful. I wish I had one.' The man headed off along the path, holding his map and smiling a big smile. Pavlov was smiling, too, and the light on his power-suit was still shining as he followed the man towards the tunnel. At the entrance he looked into the darkness, wondering if he should go in...

I haven't got time for any more of our story today. I expect we'll find out some more about what happened to Pavlov and his amazing power-suit next time, but do you remember how this story reminds us about God and things in the Bible? The first Christians lived in a very dangerous world, just like the dangerous mountain that Pavlov was on. The friends of Jesus wondered how they could survive, but God sent them some very special help.

One of those first Christians was called Philip, and one day he met an Ethiopian man who was reading a bit from the Bible about a person who was very humble and allowed himself to be killed to save others. The Ethiopian couldn't understand who this person was. Philip stopped to help, because he knew that the bit in the Bible was about Jesus.

In fact, Philip explained everything with the help of the Holy Spirit, just as Pavlov could explain the map in our story once the power-suit was connected up. Pavlov could see how all the lines worked on the map and he showed the man which path to take. The man was delighted and wished he had a suit like Pavlov's. It was the same with the Ethiopian man. He said he wanted to be like Philip—he wanted to be baptised—so that's what Philip did for him. The Ethiopian felt the power of the Holy Spirit as well.

The Bible explains what it felt like. The first Christians couldn't do anything on their own. They had to be like a 'body' together, just like Pavlov's power-suit with its different bits.

The power only worked when it was all joined up, and the first Christians were just the same. They were all joined together by God. No one was missing. When everyone was joined together, they felt an amazing power working among them.

I wonder what it was like to be Pavlov on that dangerous mountain in the snowstorm. Would you have tried to read the map? It must have been amazing when the light came on and the suit started working. And I wonder what it was like being one of those first Christians, living in a dangerous world. I wonder what it was like for Philip when he met the Ethiopian man. It must have been amazing to be all joined up like a body with the others and to feel God's power working. I wonder what it was really like. I wonder.

Possible concluding prayer

Lord God, the first Christians faced lots of dangers, but you kept them joined together and you sent a new kind of power to help them—a power that meant they could explain about Jesus to new people. Help us to be joined together with each other so that we can feel your power with us, too. Amen

Pavlov's power-suit: Week Five

Bible link

This week's Bible passage link is Acts 10:34–43, which recounts the time when the first Christians realised that Jesus loved everyone, not just the Israelites.

Key theme

This week's key theme is 'fairness'. When they really thought about it, no one in the story could come up with a good reason why only people with passes should be let into the valley. This kind of thing sometimes happens in life: people are excluded from groups and activities for unfair reasons of tradition and prejudice. Think about situations past and present, in and out of school, in which this might be the case. Think about how it feels to be excluded unfairly and how we can make sure in our own situations that people are properly included.

Episode Five

(Have the six parts of the power-suit to hand, ensuring that they are separate.)

Do you remember our story from last time? Do you remember how the power-suit worked? *('Dress' a volunteer in the suit. At this stage, the different parts are still connected only to themselves.)*

Do you remember how this story reminds us of the first Christians and how, when they were all joined up together, an amazing power was given to them?

Pavlov peered into the tunnel and then he stepped inside. His footsteps echoed around and soon it was completely dark. Every now and again, he met someone else going the same way as him. Suddenly, up ahead, he could hear lots of shouting and angry voices. As he walked forward, he could see the exit of the tunnel, where the path led into a valley, but lots of people were still in the tunnel. They seemed to be stuck.

Then Pavlov noticed a big barrier across the exit, with guards wearing uniforms and carrying weapons. They looked very fierce. People were asking to go past the barrier, and the guards were asking to see their passes. Every now and again, someone had a pass and they were let through, but most of the people didn't have passes and they were stopped. 'Can I go through, please?' Pavlov asked. 'Show us your pass,' answered one of the guards with a growl. 'I haven't got a pass,' said Pavlov. 'Then you can't go through!' said the guard.

Pavlov was very upset. 'The valley looks so nice,' he thought to himself. 'I'm sure, if I was there, I'd easily survive the whole seven days on the mountain.' But the guards wouldn't let him through, whatever he tried saying. Then Pavlov thought of his power-suit. Perhaps, if he connected it up, it would help him get past the guards. (*Move the electric plugs to different-coloured sockets so that every part of the suit is connected together. Switch the light on as the last connection is made.*)

Suddenly the light on the glove came on! Pavlov could feel the suit filling with power. He started explaining to the guards why everyone needed to go through and, as he talked, he could feel that his words were filled with power. To start with, the guards shook their heads, but gradually they started listening. When Pavlov finished talking, all the people in the tunnel cheered. Then the chief guard spoke. 'I've spent my whole life guarding this tunnel and only letting people with passes through,' he said, 'but now I've heard you explain with such powerful words, I can see that I must let everyone through!' The people all cheered again as the barrier was lifted, and Pavlov ran through with everyone else into the valley. 'This suit really has got amazing powers when I connect it all up,' he said to himself as he ran into the sunshine.

I haven't got time for any more of our story today. I expect we'll find out some more about what happened to Pavlov and his amazing power-suit next time, but do you remember how this story reminds us about God and things in the Bible? The first Christians lived in a very dangerous world, just like the dangerous mountain that Pavlov was on. The friends of Jesus wondered how they could survive, but God sent them some very special help.

To start with, the Christians were only people who came from the same country as Jesus—the Israelites—and some of those people thought it would be like that for ever. They didn't think people from other countries could be Christians, so they wouldn't let them join the church. It was a bit like in our story, when only the people with a pass could get through the barrier. Everyone else was stopped from going through. But one day Peter, who had been one of Jesus' disciples, had a vision from God, and God showed him that everyone could follow Jesus, just as Pavlov wanted everyone to get through the barrier. When Pavlov connected his power-suit, his speech was so powerful that it persuaded the guards to let everyone through, and it was the same for Peter. The Holy Spirit helped him speak very powerfully and everyone listened. After that, anyone could follow Jesus.

The Bible explains what it felt like. The first Christians couldn't do anything on their own. They had to be like a 'body' together, just like Pavlov's power-suit with its different bits. The power only worked when it was all joined up, and the first Christians were just the same. They were all joined together by God. No one was missing. When everyone was joined together, they felt an amazing power working among them.

I wonder what it was like to be Pavlov on that dangerous mountain in the snowstorm. Would you have tried persuading the guards in the tunnel? It must have been amazing when the light came on and the suit started working. And I wonder what it was like being one of those first Christians, living in a dangerous world. I wonder what it was like for Peter when he made his speech. It must have been amazing to be all joined up like a body with the others and to feel God's power working. I wonder what it was really like. I wonder.

Possible concluding prayer

Lord God, the first Christians faced lots of dangers, but you kept them joined together and you sent a new kind of power to help them—a power that helped them welcome everyone as a friend. Help us to be joined together with each other so that we can feel your power with us, too. Amen

Pavlov's power-suit: Week Six

Bible link

This week's Bible passage link is Acts 13:1–3, which recounts the time when Paul and Barnabas were sent out as apostles by the first Christians to tell everyone about Jesus.

Key theme

This week's key theme is 'getting a message across'. Pavlov needs the help of his power-suit to make his voice strong enough to shout guidance to others on the mountain. The disciples of Jesus had to travel to lots of different places to spread their message. Nowadays, we have lots of different ways of getting messages to people close by and far away. Think of all the different ways in which we can get messages to people and how this has changed the way we live.

Episode Six

(Have the six parts of the power-suit to hand, ensuring that they are separate.)

Do you remember our story from last time? Do you remember the amazing things the power-suit helped Pavlov do, once it was connected? *('Dress' a volunteer in the suit. At this stage, the different parts are still connected only to themselves.)*

Do you remember how this story reminds us of the first Christians and how, when they were all joined up together, an amazing power was given to them?

Pavlov counted up the days he'd been on the mountain. He realised it was six days now—he only had to survive for one more day, but the weather was getting worse again. Dark clouds were everywhere and bolts of lightning kept flashing through the sky. Even the valley wasn't safe. Pavlov looked up. There was only one place where the clouds didn't seem to reach, and that was the very peak of the mountain, which towered high above. It was covered in snow and it was so tall that it even reached above the storm clouds.

Pavlov knew he had to reach the summit to be safe, so he started walking up the slopes. The ground was so slippery, he could hardly stay upright, and every time he slid over, he bumped his arms or his legs on the solid ice. In the end, he didn't have the strength to get up again. 'What can I do now?' sobbed Pavlov to himself. 'I'll be stuck here. Someone will have to rescue me and I won't complete the challenge.' Then he remembered his power-suit. Perhaps, if he connected it up, it would help him escape the storm. (*Move the electric plugs to different-coloured sockets so that every part of the suit is connected together. Switch the light on as the last connection is made.*)

Suddenly the light on the glove came on! Pavlov could feel the suit filling with power. He started feeling energy flowing into his body and heard himself speaking with a powerful voice. 'Please send me up higher, power-suit!' he shouted. 'Send me higher!' Then an amazing thing happened. The power-suit started to roar like a powerful engine and, before he knew what was happening, Pavlov was flying up through the air, higher and higher. Up he soared and he landed right on the top of the mountain, up above the storm clouds. Now he was safe!

As Pavlov looked down, he could see all the other people on

the mountain still struggling in the storm. 'Come up here, to the top, above the storm!' shouted Pavlov, and the power-suit made his voice very loud. The other people could hear him. They were amazed he'd reached the top and they could see that that was where they needed to go as well. So they all began climbing up, encouraged by Pavlov's voice. 'I wonder if they'll all make it up here,' he said to himself as he watched them struggling on the ice.

Our story is almost finished now, and we'll hear one last bit about Pavlov and his amazing power-suit next time. But do you remember how this story reminds us about God and things in the Bible? The first Christians lived in a very dangerous world, just like the dangerous mountain that Pavlov was on. The friends of Jesus wondered how they could survive, but God sent them some very special help.

The first Christians soon realised that they wouldn't survive for long unless they sent out people called 'apostles' to tell everyone about Jesus, just as Pavlov in our story realised that he wouldn't survive unless the power-suit sent him up to the top of the mountain. Once, the first Christians sent out two men called Barnabas and Paul. With the power of the Holy Spirit, they told hundreds of people about Jesus, just as Pavlov shouted from the top of the mountain using the power-suit, to explain that the other people needed to come up higher as well.

In fact, Barnabas and Paul went to lots of different places and, with the help of the Holy Spirit, they took the news about Jesus to every country they knew about.

The Bible explains what it felt like. The first Christians couldn't do anything on their own. Paul explained that they had to be like a 'body' together, just like Pavlov's power-suit with its different bits. The power only worked when it was all joined up, and the first Christians were just the same. They were all joined together by God. No one was missing. When everyone was joined together, they felt an amazing power working among them.

I wonder what it was like to be Pavlov on that dangerous mountain in the snowstorm. It must have been amazing when the light came on and the suit started working. I wonder what it felt like, flying up to the top of the mountain. And I wonder what it was like being one of those first Christians, living in a dangerous world. I wonder what it was like for Barnabas and Paul when they were sent out to spread the news of Jesus. It must have been amazing to be all joined up like a body with the other Christians and to feel God's power working. I wonder what it was really like. I wonder.

Possible concluding prayer

Lord God, the first Christians faced lots of dangers, but you kept them joined together and you sent a new kind of power to help them—a power that meant they could go out into the whole world and spread the news about Jesus. Help us to be joined together with each other so that we can feel your power with us, too. Amen

Pavlov's power-suit:
Concluding celebration

The story of 'Pavlov's power-suit' can end very successfully with a Pentecost celebration. The final episode of the story acts as a reminder that the first Christians were like a 'body' all joined together with love, and the power of the Holy Spirit worked among them.

Key theme

This week's key theme is 'our school family'. Throughout this story, the main theme has been about being joined together to work together, share together and so on. For Christians, this is illustrated by the idea of everyone being part of a body and all the parts doing their own job, working in harmony. Think about how our school is a single community. What might it be like if one year group, one class or one teacher were missing? What binds us all together? How does it feel to be part of our school family?

Concluding episode

(Have the six parts of the power-suit to hand, ensuring that they are separate.)

I wonder if you remember the story of Pavlov the inventor and his power-suit. The challenge he faced was to survive on the most dangerous mountain in the world for a whole week. He'd have found it impossible if he hadn't been wearing his power-suit. *('Dress' a volunteer in the suit. At this stage, the different parts are still connected only to themselves.)*

The suit helped Pavlov talk to the weather in many different languages to calm it down, and it helped him persuade people to share things. It helped him heal an injured man and read a mysterious map. It helped him change the mind of the guards at a barrier and, last of all, it sent him right up on to the top of the mountain, out of reach of the storms. But it only worked if all the connections were made and the light came on. (*Move the electric plugs to different-coloured sockets so that every part of the suit is connected together. Switch the light on as the last connection is made.*) The suit needed to be joined up, and then its power started working.

This story reminds us of the first Christians. They were trying to survive in a dangerous world, just as Pavlov was trying to survive on the dangerous mountain. Just as Pavlov's suit only gave power when it was connected up, so the first Christians only felt the power of the Holy Spirit when they were all joined together in unity. When the Holy Spirit gave power to them, they grew in number and they did amazing things.

On the day of Pentecost, when the Holy Spirit flickered like tongues of flame on their heads, they found that they could talk in many different languages, so everyone could understand their message. Later on, they found that they could share everything they had, because the Holy Spirit stopped them being selfish. The Holy Spirit even helped Peter to heal a beggar who was very ill, and helped Philip to tell an Ethiopian man what the Bible really meant. The Holy Spirit showed the first Christians that anyone could be a friend of Jesus. Christians didn't have to come from one special country, where the Israelites lived. And the first Christians discovered that the Holy Spirit always went with them, sending them on their way wherever they went. The

Holy Spirit gave them power to do so many amazing things if they stayed joined together.

In the Bible, it says that the first Christians were joined together as if they were a body. A body needs its arms and legs and all the other parts if it is to be complete. All the parts are different and, if just one part is missing, it isn't a whole body. That's what the first Christians discovered. They needed everyone to be joined together, with no one missing. Little people and big people, old people and young people, rich people and poor people—everyone had to be there to make the body complete.

Pavlov could see everything from the top of the mountain. He was above the clouds in the sunshine, but down below he could see lots of other people struggling upwards through the wind and snow. They kept looking up and pointing to where Pavlov was standing, then they hurried on. Gradually they all made it right to the very top. 'How did you get to the mountain peak so easily?' they asked Pavlov. 'It's a hard climb, and you don't seem to be out of breath.' Pavlov showed them his power-suit. 'When I make all the connections, it gives me an amazing power,' he explained. 'It brought me safely up here to the top. But if any of the connections are broken, it stops working.' *(Unplug one of the connections and turn the light off.)*

The other people gathered around, looking at the suit. 'Can we have a turn at wearing it?' they asked, and Pavlov agreed. Every person who tried it on could feel the power working as soon as the last connection was made. *(Reconnect the suit and turn the light on.)* 'It's amazing!' they all shouted with delight. The power made them feel so happy.

The first Christians were filled with happiness as well. The

Holy Spirit helped them do amazing things together. It says in the Bible that some of them were apostles, sent out to spread the news about Jesus. Some of them were prophets. Some of them were teachers. Some of them worked miracles. Some had gifts of healing. Some helped others. Some organised everything and some of them could speak in a special language that God gave them. They were all different but they all belonged together.

Sometimes people couldn't understand how the Christians were joined together in a big family. People said you needed rules and regulations to make people become like one body, but the Christians didn't seem to have special rules. Instead they had the power of the Holy Spirit, which put the power of love into their hearts.

That's what our story about Pavlov's power-suit reminds us about. It reminds us that love can join people together and make them happy and it reminds us that God's Holy Spirit makes this possible. If we remember that, we've remembered what Pentecost really means.

*

Pavlov's power-suit:
Ideas for classroom follow-up

RE

- Read and explore the stories paralleled in the story of 'Pavlov's power-suit'.
- Explore Christian ideas about the Trinity, as illustrated in the story of Pentecost and the coming of the Holy Spirit.
- Research the Christian festival of Pentecost (also called Whitsun).
- Find out about baptism—how and why Christians are baptised in different ways.
- Discuss the concept of miracles in Christianity and other religions.
- Talk about visions and messages from God in Christianity and other religions. Examples include Bernadette at Lourdes, Lady Recheldis at Walsingham, Muhammad on the mountain, and God asking Abraham to sacrifice Isaac (in Judaism) or Ishmael (in Islam).
- Explore the idea that Christians today are the 'body of Christ'—individuals with lots of different roles doing God's work in the world. This idea links with the KS2 NSFRE theme of 'beliefs in action in the world'.

PSHE/Citizenship

- Discuss the concept of cooperation—working together for the greater good of the whole.

Geography

- Find out about a mountainous region and the impact of extreme weather conditions on the region and the lives of people there.
- Learn about maps and how to read them.

History

- Find out about the history of mountaineering and all the equipment that supports those who enjoy the sport.
- Research people who have climbed Mount Everest—those who have succeeded and those who have attempted it.
- Find historical examples of unfair or exclusive traditions being overturned—for example, women winning the right to vote; abolition of corporal punishment in schools and so on.
- Discover how communications networks have developed and changed people's lives.

Design Technology

- Investigate a range of items that are used for communication—how they are used and the impact they have on people's lives.

*

Section Six

Paul's letters

Key Bible verse

We who have this spiritual treasure are like common clay pots,
in order to show that the supreme power belongs to God,
not to us.

2 CORINTHIANS 4:7

Values

Loyalty and self-discovery

This section is designed to run between the May break and the end of the school year in July. The theme is 'Paul's letters' and, in the big story of God's love for the world, we are remembering the time when Paul wrote to different churches to explain more about how God's 'treasure' was inside people who trusted in Jesus. When we imagine ourselves within this part of the story, we discover what it feels like to get and give advice and we find out how to discover God's treasure within us.

'Hyperlink Harita' is a story told in six parts, plus a concluding episode, which illustrates some of the messages in the biblical letters that Paul wrote.

- Week One: Romans 13:1–7
- Week Two: 2 Corinthians 8:1–7
- Week Three: 1 Timothy 6:9–10
- Week Four: 1 Thessalonians 5:4–6
- Week Five: Ephesians 5:1–2
- Week Six: Galatians 3:2–5

The storyteller's prop used for 'Hyperlink Harita' consists of the 'hyperlink', which is an adapted telephone handset:

- A basic phone handset
- A loop of wire for an aerial, made from a coat-hanger, attached at the top.
- Another attachment that makes a noise and a light—for example, the handle of a toy lightsabre.

Suggested music

Suggestions for pre-recorded music that could be used at the start and end of assemblies include:

- 'I've gotta get a message to you' (Bee Gees, Reprise Records B002HFP0QU)
- 'Message in a bottle' (Gabriel Yared, Warner Bros B00000HZFQ)
- *Night on the Bare Mountain* (Mussorgsky, Naxos B00002751G)

Suggestions for songs that could be sung at assemblies include:

- Brother, sister, let me serve you
- Colours of day
- If I were a butterfly
- One more step along the world I go
- This little light of mine

Hyperlink Harita: Week One

Bible link

This week's Bible passage link is Romans 13:1–7, which records Paul's advice to the Christians living in Rome to accept the authority of the leaders and governors in the city.

Key theme

This week's key theme is 'safety'. Think about why parents, schools and clubs insist on certain kinds of behaviour or types of clothing for the sake of safety. Pupils should think of ways in which they take safety precautions—for example, bicycle helmets, protective pads for rollerskating and skateboarding, cycling proficiency training, swimming lessons and so on. Talk about the consequences for themselves and those who care about them of ignoring safety advice.

Episode One

(Have the hyperlink to hand.)

Today I want to start telling a new story. It's a story about a girl and a boy who were on an unusual kind of treasure hunt. It's a very special story because it tells us about God and about things in the Bible.

The treasure hunt was very unusual because you could only join in if you had a team of two people. Our story is about a girl called Harita and a boy called Shah who made a brilliant team because they were loyal friends. In the treasure hunt, one of the people in the team was allowed to search all round a giant adventure park for the treasure, but the other one had to stay at home. Luckily, they were allowed to use a special video link and the person searching for the treasure could press a 'help' button to get help from their friend back at home. But the only way that the friend could send help back was by using a strange machine called a 'hyperlink'. (*Show the hyperlink.*)

I wonder if you know how the hyperlink works? It has a massive memory-bank full of different messages you can send. All you have to do is enter the correct six-figure number and then press the 'send' button. For example, the message saying, 'Remember to eat your packed lunch' is number 204097. (*Demonstrate sending this message.*) Harita and Shah decided that Harita would stay at home with the hyperlink and Shah would search for the treasure.

Shah set off with lots of useful equipment in his bag. The adventure playground was an amazing place. There were pedal-karts, kayaks, sledge runs, climbing walls and loads of other things. There was a big lake and Shah thought the treasure might be on the other side, so he found a kayak. Harita was watching everything using the live video link. Some grown-ups were organising the kayaks and told Shah that he must wear a lifejacket and do a practice capsize drill. At first, Shah thought that would slow him down and that the grown-ups were bossing him around too much, but he decided to ask Harita for advice by pressing the 'help' button.

Harita looked through the menu of messages she could send using the hyperlink. There was one that said, 'Pretend you're a fish and swim across the lake.' Harita remembered that Shah wasn't a very good swimmer, so she found another message in the memory-bank. It said, 'Grab the biggest kayak and go while no one's looking.' She started entering the numbers, but then she remembered about the lifejacket and the capsize drill. She searched the hyperlink again and another message flashed up: 'Do as the grown-ups tell you.'

'It seems a bit boring,' thought Harita to herself, 'but friends are supposed to be loyal and help one another.' So she sent the message advising Shah to do as the grown-ups were telling him. (*Send the message using the hyperlink.*) Shah read the message. Then he put on the lifejacket and did the capsize drill, as the grown-ups had said. Quickly he paddled off over the lake in search of the treasure, but when he was halfway across he suddenly noticed a massive whirlpool up ahead, sucking everything down. He was being dragged closer and closer...

I haven't got time for any more of my story today. Next time we'll hear some more, but it's a very special story because it tells us something important about God and Jesus. Harita's hyperlink reminds us about the apostle Paul and the letters he wrote. Harita could only use the hyperlink to send messages to her friend Shah, and Paul could only send letters to his friends, who were all around the cities he'd visited.

Harita gave advice to Shah, just as Paul gave advice to his friends. Harita wanted Shah to find the treasure in the treasure hunt, and Paul wanted his friends to find a special, true kind of 'treasure' that God gives. Harita sent a message to Shah, telling him to do as the grown-ups said, and once Paul wrote a letter to the people living in Rome. In it he told them that they should obey the city authorities. Although it felt as if the authorities were bossing them around, in the end that was the best thing for Paul's friends, to help them find God's treasure. It was just like the grown-ups who knew that Shah had to wear a lifejacket and practise the capsize drill if he was going to find the treasure in the treasure hunt.

You can actually read Paul's letters still, in the Bible. They were all like messages sending help to other people and telling them about God and Jesus. In all his messages, Paul told his friends about the treasure that fills our lives with happiness.

I wonder what it was like to be Shah or Harita. What messages would you have sent? How would you have felt, looking for the treasure? I wonder what it was like getting one of Paul's letters and hearing the advice in his message. It must have been great, discovering about the real treasure inside us and finding out ways to be like Jesus. I wonder if the people listened to what Paul said. I wonder if you would have followed Paul's advice and found the treasure. I wonder.

Possible concluding prayer

Lord God, Paul wrote lots of letters to his friends so that he could give them advice and help them find the treasure you give. Help us to be loyal friends and help us to discover your treasure in our lives. Amen

*

Hyperlink Harita: Week Two

Bible link

This week's Bible passage link is 2 Corinthians 8:1–7, which records Paul's advice to the Christians living in Corinth that they should always give generously.

Key theme

This week's key theme is 'giving generously'. Christians believe that it is important to share what they have and not keep everything for themselves. One of the ways in which they do this is by supporting charities, either with money or with their time. Think about any charities and initiatives that the school supports. Discuss which ones different people feel most strongly about and why. Do pupils think it is important to support other people in these ways? Why?

Episode Two

(Have the hyperlink to hand.)

I wonder if you remember anything about the story we began last time. What were the names of the two people in the team? How could they send messages? *(Show the hyperlink and send a test message.)*

Do you remember what this story reminds us of in the Bible? Can you remember how the apostle Paul sent letters to all his friends to give them advice?

Shah was very good at paddling the kayak across the lake, but he soon realised that the whirlpool was sucking him closer and closer. However hard he paddled, he couldn't escape. 'Help me!' he shouted, but no one heard. Suddenly the kayak was dragged under by the rushing water and Shah was in the lake. He thought he'd drown but his lifejacket kept him safe. In the end he reached a little island with a few trees, right in the middle of the lake. There were other people on the island but Shah was worried to discover that they were all on the treasure hunt as well. Everyone was hoping they would be the one to find the treasure first, but they were all stuck on the island.

Shah looked in his bag and found some rope. 'What can I do?' he asked himself, and then he remembered his friend Harita with the hyperlink. He pressed his 'help' button. Straight away Harita started looking through the menu on the hyperlink. After searching for a few minutes, she found a message that said, 'Tie the rope to a tree and use it as a lifeline.' It seemed like a good idea, but Harita guessed that the rope wouldn't be long enough to reach the edge of the lake, so she kept on searching. The next message she found said, 'Make a glider and fly to escape.' She was about to enter the number on the hyperlink when she remembered that Shah wasn't very good at tying knots. She was worried that his glider would fall apart. Just then, she spotted another message: 'Cut the rope up into bits and share it.'

Harita frowned. The other people were all searching for the treasure as well. Why should Shah share with them? But she had a feeling that this was the message she must send, so she entered the number and sent the message on the hyperlink. *(Send the message using the hyperlink.)* As Shah started cutting his rope up and sharing it, the other people were amazed at his generosity. Gradually they got other things out of their bags as well—a saw to cut wood and a sheet to make a sail. Before long, they'd made a fine raft and set out for the edge of the lake together.

As they were crossing the water, Shah saw glinting metal up on a faraway hill, shining in the sunlight. 'That must be the treasure!' he said to himself. He quickly looked in his bag for his map, to try to see which hill it was, but when he next looked up, the sun had gone in and the glinting had stopped. Before long, the raft landed at the edge of the lake. Shah and the others jumped on to the landing stage. There were three paths ahead of them but Shah didn't know which one was best to take...

I haven't got time for any more of our story today. Next time we'll hear some more, but it's a very special story because it tells us something important about God and Jesus. Harita's hyperlink reminds us about the apostle Paul and the letters he wrote. Harita had to use the hyperlink to send messages to her friend Shah, and Paul sent letters to his friends, who were all around the cities he'd visited.

Harita gave advice to Shah, just as Paul gave advice to his friends. Harita wanted Shah to find the treasure in the treasure hunt, and Paul wanted his friends to find a special, true kind of 'treasure' that God gives. In our story, Harita sent a message to Shah, telling him to share the rope and be generous, and once Paul wrote a letter to some people called the Corinthians. In it he told them that they should be generous, always sharing everything they had, because then they would be acting like God. That's the best thing to do if you're going to find God's treasure. It's just like when Shah discovered that sharing the rope meant he could build a raft with the other people and carry on with the treasure hunt.

You can actually read Paul's letters still, in the Bible. They were all like messages, sending help to other people and telling them about God and Jesus. In all his messages, Paul told his friends about the treasure that fills our lives with happiness.

I wonder what it was like to be Shah or Harita. What messages would you have sent? How would you have felt if you'd been Shah, sharing your rope with other people even though they were hunting for the treasure as well? And I wonder what it was like getting one of Paul's letters and hearing the advice in his message. It must have been great, discovering about the real treasure inside us and finding out ways to be like Jesus. I wonder if the people listened to what Paul said. I wonder.

Possible concluding prayer

Lord God, Paul wrote lots of letters to his friends so that he could give them advice and help them find the treasure you give. Help us to be loyal friends and help us to discover your treasure in our lives. Amen

Hyperlink Harita: Week Three

Bible link

This week's Bible passage link is 1 Timothy 6:9–10, which records Paul's advice to his friend Timothy, not to strive for more money.

Key theme

This week's key theme is 'wealth'. Accumulating prizes did not help Shah in his treasure hunt. Think about the importance of money and valuable things to a contented life. Is money what makes people most happy on their way through life? What might be more important? Why? This theme will link with the previous week's theme on giving generously and will enable further development of ideas about how giving can actually bring pleasure to the giver.

Episode Three

(Have the hyperlink to hand.)

I wonder if you remember anything about our story from last time. How did Shah and Harita send messages to each other? *(Show the hyperlink and send a test message.)*

Do you remember what this story reminds us of in the Bible? Can you remember how the apostle Paul sent letters to all his friends, to give them advice?

Shah looked at the three paths, but they all looked the same. Suddenly the sun came out from behind a cloud and he saw a glinting light shining up on one of the hills. One of the paths led in that direction so Shah quickly set off down it. After ten minutes, the path brought him to a funfair. There were rides and stalls everywhere so Shah had a look around. One of the stalls had a game where you threw three balls through a hoop. The prize was a huge bag of gold coins so Shah decided to have a go. He threw the balls one by one, and won the prize. The bag of coins went into his backpack and he carried on looking round the fair.

Soon Shah found a stall where you had to throw three hoops over a funny-shaped statue. The statue was solid gold and, if you got all three hoops over it, you won it. His first hoop went over the statue perfectly and his second was the same. Carefully he threw the third hoop, and over it went. He'd won the solid gold statue. He put it into his backpack and staggered off—the prizes were very heavy.

Then Shah saw another stall, where you had to swing a hammer down as hard as you could to ring a bell. You were allowed three tries to win a big golden cup with jewels all over it. Lots of strong people had a go, but no one could do it. Shah knew he was strong as well and, on his third try, he managed to ring the bell and win the cup. He put it in his backpack and set off to find the pathway, but his pack was so heavy, he couldn't move more than one step. He didn't know what to do so he decided to ask Harita for help.

Harita looked through the menu on the hyperlink. The first message she found said, 'Sell the prizes back to the stall-holders.' It sounded like a good idea, but she looked some more and found another one: 'Bury the prizes in the ground and come back for them later.' That sounded even better but she kept searching through the menu. Just then, a very strange message popped up: 'Give all the prizes to someone else.'

Harita thought carefully about how the prizes had stopped Shah moving. In the end, she decided to tell Shah to give the prizes away. (*Send the message using the hyperlink.*) Shah noticed some very poor people who didn't have enough money to go to the funfair, so he gave the prizes to them. They were so pleased and kept saying 'thank you' to him. Shah smiled a big smile. All that weight was gone and he could walk quickly again, to carry on with the treasure hunt. So he searched for the pathway, but he couldn't find it anywhere…

I haven't got time for any more of our story today. Next time we'll hear some more, but it's a very special story because it tells us something important about God and Jesus. Harita's hyperlink reminds us about the apostle Paul and the letters he wrote. Harita had to use the hyperlink to send messages to her friend Shah, and Paul sent letters to his friends, who were all around the cities he'd visited.

Harita gave advice to Shah, just as Paul gave advice to his friends. Harita wanted Shah to find the treasure in the treasure hunt, and Paul wanted his friends to find a special, true kind of 'treasure' that God gives. Today, in our story, Harita sent a message to Shah, telling him to give his heavy prizes away so that they didn't weigh him down.

Once, Paul wrote a letter to a friend of his called Timothy. In the letter he told Timothy not to try to get lots of money and gold, because it would stop him being close to God. It was true for Timothy and it's true for everyone who wants to find God's treasure. It's just like when Shah gave his golden prizes away and found that he could carry on with his search.

You can actually read Paul's letters still, in the Bible. They were all like messages, sending help to other people and telling them about God and Jesus. In all his messages, Paul told his friends about the treasure that fills our lives with happiness.

I wonder what it was like to be Shah or Harita. What messages would you have sent? How would you have felt if you'd been Shah, winning those prizes and then giving them away? And I wonder what it was like getting one of Paul's letters and hearing the advice in his message. It must have been great, discovering about the real treasure inside us and finding out ways to be like Jesus. I wonder if the people listened to what Paul said. I wonder.

Possible concluding prayer

Lord God, Paul wrote lots of letters to his friends so that he could give them advice and help them find the treasure you give. Help us to be loyal friends and help us to discover your treasure in our lives. Amen

*

Hyperlink Harita: Week Four

Bible link

This week's Bible passage link is 1 Thessalonians 5:4–6, which records Paul's advice to the Christians living in Thessalonica, that they should always stay alert, ready for God to reveal his plans to them.

Key theme

This week's key theme is 'concentration'. Sometimes, when we are supposed to be doing school work or a job for parents, we get distracted. We forget what we are supposed to be doing or we begin to think it will be all right to put it off. Talk about times when this has happened and about the consequences. Think about why it is difficult to concentrate or stay with the task. What can help us in times like this? What does it mean to be self-disciplined? What are the advantages of concentrating on a task?

Episode Four

(Have the hyperlink to hand.)

I wonder if you remember anything about our story from last time. What messages has Harita sent to Shah? *(Show the hyperlink and send a test message.)*

Do you remember what this story reminds us of in the Bible? Can you remember how the apostle Paul sent letters to all his friends, to give them advice?

Shah hunted around the funfair for ages, looking for the path, but it seemed to have disappeared. He knew he needed to find the path, and the more he looked, the more worried he got. He started asking other people but they were all too busy enjoying themselves. 'I'm on an important treasure hunt!' he explained to everyone he met, but no one was interested. Soon he was desperate and tears started coming into his eyes, but the other people just laughed at him or shrugged their shoulders. Just then, Shah spotted a tent with a big sign outside.

It was a fortune-teller's tent and the sign said, 'I will help you find things you've lost and know about things that are yet to come.' Shah went into the tent. It was dark and there were some candles flickering. There was also a nice smell in the air, which reminded him somehow of bedtime. Some gentle, soothing music played in the background. He sat down on a chair and waited.

Shah began to feel very sleepy. His eyes kept closing and he had to force himself to stay awake, but then a strange woman appeared. She was wearing a long flowing robe and had a big scarf wrapped around her hair. She smiled at Shah and said, 'Tell me what you are looking for and I will help you see it.' Shah started talking about the treasure and the path. The woman smiled at him again and said, 'Don't worry! That treasure might not be real after all. Anyway, there's no rush. There are other things that are more important.' All the time, the gentle music was playing and the tent was growing darker. Shah felt his eyes closing and, about three minutes later, he was fast asleep in the chair.

Harita could see everything that was going on. She was very worried. Shah seemed to be giving up the treasure hunt altogether. He had fallen asleep instead of concentrating on staying alert and awake. How could she help? She searched desperately through the menu of the hyperlink. There were lots of good messages about eating enough vegetables every day and doing enough exercise, but none of them would help Shah just now. Finally she found the one she needed. The code number was 999999 and the message was simply, 'Wake up!' So she tried sending the message. *(Pretend to be Shah, asleep on a chair, and get three children to try to send the message using the hyperlink.)*

Harita was about to give up, but, just when she was trying for the last time, Shah began to wake up. He could hear the hyperlink and he could see the message saying, 'Wake up!' He remembered the treasure and he jumped up and ran out of the tent. He had to find the path—and there it was! It was very hard to see, but it led off through some trees towards a big hill. So he ran as fast as he could along the path…

I haven't got time for any more of our story today. Next time we'll hear some more, but it's a very special story because it tells us something important about God and Jesus. Harita's hyperlink reminds us about the apostle Paul and the letters he wrote. Harita had to use the hyperlink to send messages to her friend Shah, and Paul sent letters to his friends, who were all around the cities he'd visited.

Harita gave advice to Shah, just as Paul gave advice to his friends. Harita wanted Shah to find the treasure in the treasure hunt, and Paul wanted his friends to find a special, true kind of 'treasure' that God gives. In our story today, Harita had to send an emergency message to Shah, telling him to wake up quickly and stay alert.

One of the letters Paul wrote was to the Christians in a city in

Greece called Thessalonica. In his letter, Paul told them to stay alert and ready for the time when God would show them his plans. He gave them this message because he wanted them to find God's true treasure. It's just like when Harita had to send her emergency message to Shah, to wake him up so that he could carry on with his search.

You can actually read Paul's letters still, in the Bible. They were all like messages, sending help to other people and telling them about God and Jesus. In all his messages, Paul told his friends about the treasure that fills our lives with happiness.

I wonder what it was like to be Shah or Harita. What messages would you have sent? If you'd been Harita, would you have panicked when you saw Shah fast asleep? And I wonder what it was like getting one of Paul's letters and hearing the advice in his message. It must have been great, discovering about the real treasure inside us and finding out ways to be like Jesus. I wonder if the people listened to what Paul said. I wonder.

Possible concluding prayer

Lord God, Paul wrote lots of letters to his friends so that he could give them advice and help them find the treasure you give. Help us to be loyal friends and help us to discover your treasure in our lives. Amen

*

Hyperlink Harita: Week Five

Bible link

This week's Bible passage link is Ephesians 5:1–2, which records Paul's advice to the Christians living in Ephesus, telling them to be like Jesus, who was willing to sacrifice himself for others because he loved them so much.

Key theme

This week's key theme is 'sacrifice'. Explore different forms of sacrifice. Talk about times when pupils have made sacrifices for others and when others have made sacrifices for them. How do these experiences feel?

Episode Five

(Have the hyperlink to hand.)

I wonder if you remember anything about our story from last time. Can you remember the message that Harita had to send to Shah? *(Show the hyperlink and send a test message.)*

Do you remember what this story reminds us of in the Bible? Can you remember how the apostle Paul sent letters to all his friends, to give them advice?

Shah was so relieved that he'd found the path again. He walked quickly along it and came round a corner. There was a big sign saying 'Treasure Trove Adventure Park, only three miles'. 'I'm really close to the treasure now,' Shah said to himself as he went past the sign. Soon, another sign said, '... only two miles to go'. A bit further along, another sign said that it was only one mile away. Shah was practically running now, and when he came round the next corner he could see the adventure park. It had climbing ropes, slides and chutes, balancing beams and little dens that you could hide in, but all of it was hanging from enormous ropes that came down the side of a cliff. The whole adventure park was up in the air and no one seemed to be playing on it at all.

Then Shah noticed a ladder that went up from the ground to the bottom layer of the adventure park. A crowd was at the bottom of the ladder. Shah asked them why they weren't going up and one of them explained, 'There's a gap halfway up the ladder. No one can get up.' Sure enough, there was a place where five of the rungs were missing. The gap was big but Shah was tall enough to stretch out his fingers and touch the next rung. The other people cheered, 'You can make it!' But Shah could see that they were sad because they weren't tall enough to bridge the gap. He looked up again. The adventure playground looked great and somewhere up there was the treasure, but the ladder was creaking and groaning badly. It felt as if it would collapse at any minute. Should he risk swinging up over the gap or not? He wasn't sure so he decided to ask Harita for help.

Harita had been watching Shah carefully so she quickly looked through the menu on the hyperlink to find the right message to send. Soon she found a message saying, 'Come back down straight away—the ladder is dangerous.' She knew that would be the safest thing to say, but she kept looking some more. Another message said, 'Reach up over the gap and climb up quickly.' She was about to send it when she spotted the very next message on the menu: 'Make a human bridge over the gap and let the others climb over you.' Harita thought to herself. Then she decided to tell Shah to make a human bridge, to let the others climb up over him. (*Send the message using the hyperlink.*)

Shah heard the message and straight away he made the bridge. The other people all scrambled over and Shah grew weaker and weaker. Just as the last person had climbed over, he could feel his fingers slipping. He tried to hold on but he couldn't. The ladder was crumbling away into pieces and Shah was falling down and down...

Next time we'll hear what happened to Shah, but I'm sure you remember that our story is very special because it tells us something important about God and Jesus. Harita's hyperlink reminds us about the apostle Paul and the letters he wrote. Harita had to use the hyperlink to send messages to her friend Shah, and Paul sent letters to his friends, who were all around the cities he'd visited.

Harita gave advice to Shah, just as Paul gave advice to his friends. Harita wanted Shah to find the treasure in the treasure hunt, and Paul wanted his friends to find a special, true kind of 'treasure' that God gives. In our story today, Harita decided to send a message to Shah, telling him to make a human bridge so that he could help others get up the ladder.

One of the letters that Paul wrote was to the Christians in a city called Ephesus. In his letter, Paul told them to copy Jesus, who loved people so much that he even gave up his own life to save them. Paul gave them this message because he wanted them to find God's true treasure. It's just like when Harita told

Shah to make a human bridge to help the others, even if he risked his own safety.

You can still read Paul's letters in the Bible. They were all like hyperlink messages, sending help to other people and telling them about God and Jesus. In all his messages, Paul told his friends about the treasure that fills our lives with happiness.

I wonder what it was like to be Shah or Harita. What messages would you have sent? If you'd been Shah, how would you have felt when all the other people used you as a human bridge? And I wonder what it was like getting one of Paul's letters and hearing the advice in his message. It must have been great, discovering about the real treasure inside us and finding out ways to be like Jesus. I wonder if the people listened to what Paul said. I wonder.

Possible concluding prayer

Lord God, Paul wrote lots of letters to his friends so that he could give them advice and help them find the treasure you give. Help us to be loyal friends and help us to discover your treasure in our lives. Amen

Hyperlink Harita: Week Six

Bible link

This week's Bible passage link is Galatians 3:2–5, which records Paul's advice to the Christians living in Galatia, that they had to make a 'leap of faith' and not just rely on being nice if they were to find God's true treasure.

Key theme

This week's key theme is 'taking risks'. Some people like adventure, risk-taking and extreme sports. Others prefer to play safe. Think about what kind of person you are. Does it matter which of the two you are? Have you ever taken risks? When might it be necessary to do so? What is the difference between taking a risk and reckless behaviour? How do you think you would have coped in Shah's situation? Was the treasure worth the risk?

Episode Six

(Have the hyperlink to hand.)

I wonder if you remember anything about our story from last time. What has happened to Shah? Do you think he'll ever find the treasure? *(Show the hyperlink and send a test message.)*

Do you remember what this story reminds us of in the Bible? Can you remember how the apostle Paul sent letters to all his friends, to give them advice?

Shah fell down and down the side of the cliff. He tried grabbing hold of the rocks as he fell, but his hands just got cut and bruised. Down he went, falling faster and faster. He could see one last little outcrop of rock and he grabbed desperately for it. Somehow he held on with his fingers. Gradually he pulled himself up on to the little outcrop. All around him was just thin air and, as the wind blew, he felt very unsafe.

Then Shah noticed an entrance to a tunnel in the cliff nearby. Although it was quite close, there was a gap between him and the hole—a gap so deep that he couldn't possibly survive it. Suddenly a mysterious person appeared at the mouth of the hole and said, 'Leap over here and you will find the treasure!'

Shah tried to stand up but the wind was blowing and the gap was very deep. However much he tried to get to his feet, he just couldn't. He was frozen, holding on to the rock as tightly as he could. Then Shah started to get angry. He shouted at the person in the tunnel, 'I've done everything right! Whenever Harita sent me a message, I did what she said. I listened to the grown-ups and did the capsize drill. I shared my rope. I didn't let all that money stop me. I woke up just in time. I even made myself into a bridge to help others get up the ladder. Why can't I just have the treasure now?' But the person in the tunnel just said again, 'Leap over here and you will find the treasure.'

Harita had been watching and she knew that Shah needed help. She looked through the menu on the hyperlink to find the right message to send. Right at the end of the list, she found one saying, 'Concentrate hard and make yourself jump across the gap.' It sounded like a good idea, but Harita kept looking. The next message she found said, 'Order the person in the tunnel to put a bridge across.' Somehow she didn't think that would work, but then she spotted one last idea on the hyperlink: 'Imagine there's no gap, and jump.' Harita started entering the number, telling Shah to imagine he was somewhere safe with no gap, and to jump. *(Send the message using the hyperlink.)*

Shah was very surprised and angry to get the message. He shouted at the person in the tunnel again: 'Help me! Make a bridge across!' But the person disappeared up the tunnel. Then Shah tried to force himself to stand up, but the gap looked so dangerous that he couldn't. In the end, he looked again at the message Harita had sent. He half-closed his eyes and imagined he was in a garden. Lovely soft grass was all around him. All he had to do was to make a perfectly safe jump across the grass...

So he jumped—and there he was in the tunnel. He'd made the leap. He scrambled up the underground passage, rushing towards the treasure. When he came out at the top of the hill, he stopped in amazement. Everything was coloured gold. It looked as though there was treasure everywhere. He reached about with his hands but he couldn't grasp anything. Then he looked down at himself. He could see that his whole body was shining gold as well. He had a wonderful feeling inside. Whenever he moved, everything seemed just right. 'This is the best kind of treasure you could ever have!' he shouted with delight.

Back at home, Harita was cheering as well. She knew that all her messages had worked. She could see Shah and she knew he'd found the treasure. She knew it was the best kind of treasure in the whole world.

Our story is just about ended now, but we might have time for one final bit. I hope you remember how Harita's hyperlink reminds us about the apostle Paul and the letters he wrote.

Harita gave advice to Shah, just as Paul gave advice to his friends. In our story today, Harita had to send a message to Shah, telling him to make a leap of faith. It was a bit like one of the letters Paul wrote, to the Christians in a place called Galatia. In his letter, Paul told them that they couldn't rely on their own bravery or even on being nice if they wanted to find God. Instead, they had to make a leap of faith. They had to believe and trust in Jesus. Then they would find the true treasure that fills people's lives with happiness.

I wonder what it was like to be Shah or Harita. If you'd been Shah, could you have made that leap of faith? And if Paul had written to you, telling you to believe and trust in Jesus and to make a leap of faith, what would you have done? I wonder.

Possible concluding prayer

Lord God, Paul wrote lots of letters to his friends so that he could give them advice and help them find the treasure you give. Help us to be loyal friends and help us to discover your treasure in our lives. Amen

Hyperlink Harita: Concluding celebration

The end of the story of 'Hyperlink Harita' coincides with the end of the school year. It is designed to be used at a leavers' service or celebration. The concluding episode reminds us that we too can have the treasure that God gives, and it will change our lives. The six stories told throughout the year all join together to make one big story, and, as we imagine ourselves within this story, so we recognise the treasure within us.

Key theme

This week's key theme is 'individual worth'. Everyone is unique and special. Think about what makes each of the people in your group or class special. Think back over the school year and what it has given you. Think how it has enabled you to grow in understanding and as a person. Think of the opportunities you've had. Think about what you have brought to your class and school. Year 6 pupils could think about how they hope to be remembered at their primary school and how they want to be seen when they go on to secondary school.

Concluding episode

(Have the six props from throughout the year to hand.)

Do you remember the story of Harita's hyperlink? *(Show the hyperlink and send a test message.)* In the end, her friend Shah made it to the top of the hill and found the treasure, but it was very unexpected treasure. He couldn't put it in his backpack. It was treasure that made him glow inside. It made him feel completely happy and peaceful.

Just as Harita sent messages so that Shah could find the treasure, so the apostle Paul wrote letters to people so that they could find the true treasure that God gives. Paul described it like this in one of his letters: 'We who have this spiritual treasure are like common clay pots.' We are like clay pots, because a clay pot doesn't look special from the outside, but inside there could be something very precious. Paul said that we have God's treasure inside us, just like Shah's treasure in our story.

Paul said that God puts his treasure inside us because he loves us. In fact, God has always loved his people. All the stories we've heard this school year reminded us about that.

(*Show Grandad's cereal box.*) Do you remember this? Who did it belong to? What did he use it for? (*Shake the box.*) Grandad managed to escape from the island where he'd been shipwrecked by using the cereal box, although he had lots of adventures on the way. And the story of Grandad's cereal box reminded us of Moses and the Israelites, who escaped from slavery in Egypt. They were God's special people but he knew they needed somewhere to go and live.

(*Show the five block-blast foam shapes.*) Do you remember the sport that these foam shapes are used for? (*Construct a simple weapon.*) The Iron City team managed to win the Milky Way Cup, and the story of their victory reminded us how Joshua and the Israelites captured the promised land. They defended it well and kept worshipping God. Do you remember how Tiny Tron imagined someone in his family, a long time later, who would look at the trophy and would go on to be the best block-blast player ever? In the promised land there was a place called Bethlehem and, a long time later, God sent his own Son, Jesus, to be born there. Jesus would be the greatest king ever known.

(*Show the pioneer's drum.*) Do you remember this drum? (*Play the rhythm of 'Will you come and follow me?'.*) What happened on the river as the pioneer took his followers to find its source? It was a journey full of adventures and it reminded us of Jesus and his disciples. They followed him everywhere and, in the end, he showed them the power that God uses to give life. Jesus still wants people to follow him and tell everyone about him. That's what his disciples do.

(*Show the judgment scales, with the bread weighing less than the weight.*) What do you remember about these weighing scales? Who wanted to pass the test to become a chef? Gaston tried cooking all sorts of things, but he was too proud to ask the cleaner for help and he kept failing the test. In the end, he did ask the cleaner, who was just a servant, to help. The cleaner helped Gaston make some bread and broke it open to show how light it was. Then Gaston passed the test and got his name in the Book of Chefs. This story reminded us how people need Jesus to help them. He is a servant-king, but it's only if we ask for his help that we can possibly pass God's test. We know about the help Jesus gives because he took some bread and broke it, and he died for us on the cross. (*Turn the scales into a cross.*)

(*Show the power-suit.*) Whose suit is this? What challenge did Pavlov face? Can you remember how Pavlov felt a wonderful power when he joined the suit up so that all the connections were made? (*Join some of the connections.*) It helped him survive on the dangerous mountain. It was a story that reminded us of the first Christians, who lived in a dangerous world. They discovered that if they stayed joined up together, they received the power of the Holy Spirit from God. That power helped them survive and it helped them grow in number as well, until there were churches everywhere.

(*Show the hyperlink.*) Harita used the hyperlink to send messages to her friend Shah so that he could find the treasure. (*Send a message.*) The hyperlink reminded us of the letters that Paul wrote. He sent messages to as many people as he could, telling them about everything God has done and telling them about the true treasure that God gives.

Our stories this year have reminded us of different things God did, but he's still doing things to help people and he helps us as well if we want him to. Some people are about to leave our school, and God will help them if they make sure they're part of his story. Some people will be back in September, and God will help them, too. We are all like clay pots filled with God's treasure, the true treasure that makes us shine.

*

Hyperlink Harita:
Ideas for classroom follow-up

RE

- Find out about the apostle Paul and the people and places to which he wrote letters.

Citizenship/RE

- Consider ways in which Christians respond to being members of a wider society, including thoughts on being law-abiding and how to offer challenge to government when we think it has got things wrong.

English/RE

- Read a children's version of *The Pilgrim's Progress* by John Bunyan. YouTube has a series of animated film clips telling the story: see www.youtube.com/watch?v=Jwlf8g0ofFo&feature=channel
- Read stories that illustrate the idea of sacrifice—for example, *Dogger* by Shirley Hughes (Red Fox, 2009) or (from the Buddhist tradition) the story of the Monkey King (see www.clear-vision.org/Students/handbook/monkey.aspx)

English

- Write letters of different types for different situations.
- Write stories about adventures in adventure parks or on treasure hunts.

Geography/History

- Find out about some of the places to which Paul's letters were sent.

Template

God's Storyteller badge

*

Bible index

Old Testament

New Testament

*

Index of values and key themes

Values

Key themes

Also by Edward J. Carter

Story Assemblies for the School Year

36 assemblies with five-minute stories, teacher's notes and RE follow-up

This book is full of memorable stories, designed to engage and delight pupils at primary level. The stories are essentially parables about God and the events in the Bible, creatively told to help children understand the big story of God's love for the world.

There are six themes in total, each with its own easy-to-make storytelling prop. The stories within each theme are divided into six weekly episodes. Together the stories cover the whole school year. At the end of each half-term there is a special assembly to mark that part of the school year: harvest, Christmas, Christingle or Pancake Day, Holy Week or Easter, Pentecost, and a leavers' farewell.

As well as being ideal for collective worship, there are practical follow-up ideas for the classroom.

The six themes cover:

- God's creation
- The message of the Old Testament prophets
- Stories about Christian values
- The story of Holy Week and Easter
- Jesus' resurrection and ascension
- The journeys of the apostle Paul

ISBN 978 0 85746 227 5   £8.99
Available from your local Christian bookshop or direct from BRF: please visit www.barnabasinschools.org.uk.

Stories for Interactive Assemblies

15 story-based assemblies to get children talking

Nigel Bishop

Collective worship is an ideal time to combine biblical teaching with contemporary storytelling. The 15 easy-to-tell, contemporary stories in this book are all based in the world of the classroom but have their roots in the parables of Jesus. Primary children of all ages will recognise themselves and their classmates in the stories and, even if they do not recognise the original story, they are invited to relate to the underlying message that is the essence of the parable.

Each story is followed by questions for the assembly or classroom, designed to help the children interact with some of the issues raised, plus suggestions for practical activities, based on different learning styles. Each story also includes:

- A target theme to help direct the teacher towards the main teaching objective.
- A prayer or reflection to close the assembly if desired.
- Bible references for the original parables.
- Information to link the teaching to PSHE/Citizenship and the non-statutory national framework for RE or local SACRE guidelines.

ISBN 978 0 85746 143 8   £6.99
Available from your local Christian bookshop or direct from BRF: please visit www.barnabasinschools.org.uk.

Also from BRF/Barnabas

More Stories for Interactive Assemblies

20 story-based assemblies to get children talking

Nigel Bishop

More Stories for Interactive Assemblies contains 20 short stories about a group of children from a typical primary school who head off to a farm for a residential visit. The stories follow the children's progress, describing their adventures, their discoveries about themselves and others, and the many ways in which they grow through their experiences.

Each story is stand-alone, although the series fits together into a chronological account. Each chapter includes a brief indication as to what the story is about, a small number of questions designed to encourage pupils to be more receptive, and an optional prayer for use in Collective Worship.

The book can also be used as a class-reader with older children, and contains an appendix of PSHE and RE links to extend the teaching and understanding of the underlying themes.

ISBN 978 1 84101 837 9   UK £7.99
Available from your local Christian bookshop or direct from BRF: please visit www.barnabasinschools.org.uk.

Assemblies for Spring and Summer Festivals

36 ready-to-use ideas for key Christian festivals and other special days

Martin Cox

This book is packed with 36 tried-and-tested assembly ideas, designed to resource the second and third terms of the school year. The ideas fall under four main themes: 'Saints of Britain', 'Faith in action', 'The life of Jesus' and 'Special days and celebrations'.

There is a wealth of material to choose from within each theme. The assemblies can be used either in date order or as a set of assemblies on one of the key themes. For completeness, cross-curricular links for the classroom are included with each theme.

Each assembly includes key background information for the teacher, key Bible stories with further Bible links, suggestions for visual aids, and creative ideas for exploring the theme including interactive storytelling, drama, songs and prayers.

ISBN 978 1 84101 701 3   £8.99
Available from your local Christian bookshop or direct from BRF: please visit www.barnabasinschools.org.uk.

Story Assemblies of 24 Saints

24 off-the-peg assembly plans for the school year

Heather Butler

Story Assemblies of 24 Saints features a wealth of saints' days spread across the school year from September to July, making it an ideal ongoing resource and enabling teachers to opt in at any time.

The material contains 24 complete assembly plans ready for teachers to pick off the shelf and deliver as a whole-school, year-group or classroom assembly.

Each outline comprises a creative mix of elements, designed to highlight a special feature about the saint and help children use their imaginations to ground the story. Topical links are included to encourage children to think about what the message of the story might mean to their own lives today.

ISBN 978 1 84101 703 7   £7.99
Available from your local Christian bookshop or direct from BRF: please visit www.barnabasinschools.org.uk.

Eyewitness Assemblies

15 ready-to-use assemblies for Easter to Pentecost

Gaynor Cobb

From Palm Sunday to Pentecost, *Eyewitness Assemblies* presents 15 short stories giving imaginative 'first-hand' accounts told from the perspective of a character in the original Bible story. The eyewitness account is followed by a reflective poem, role-play or news report to help spark children's imagination and enable them to get under the skin of the story. Each unit is stand-alone, while giving a clear and comprehensive picture of the part of the Christian story that led to Jesus' death and resurrection and the birth of the early Church.

Teacher's notes provide background information, Bible references, discussion starters and focused links into PSHE/Citizenship and RE, so that the assemblies can be followed up in class. This may be of particular use where the assembly forms part of the RE syllabus. There is also a helpful glossary and Bible index.

ISBN 978 1 84101 496 8   £7.99
Available from your local Christian bookshop or direct from BRF: please visit www.barnabasinschools.org.uk.

More Collective Worship Unwrapped

20 tried-and-tested story-based assemblies for primary schools

John Guest

More Collective Worship Unwrapped is a flexible and practical resource ideal for all teachers seeking to grasp the key principles of collective worship as quickly and as effectively as possible. The material is equally valuable for both newly qualified and experienced teachers, as well as RE coordinators and those invited into schools to lead collective worship.

Each of the 20 story-based assemblies gives a Bible base, tips on presentation, visual aids required, recommended songs, an optional prayer and follow-up material.

Each outline can be set in the context of a variety of topical themes, including moral and personal development, citizenship, spiritual values, seasons of the Christian year and special times.

ISBN 978 1 84101 664 1   £12.99
Available from your local Christian bookshop or direct from BRF: please visit www.barnabasinschools.org.uk.

The Barnabas Schools' Bible

Including Bible encyclopedia

Rhona Davies

Illustrated by Marcin Piwowarski

This new Children's Bible includes stories chosen to cover all the main events, retold with a continuous thread.

There are 365 stories, one for every day of the year, each accompanied by Bible quotations from a real Bible translation, giving readers a taste of the language and style of the original texts.

The stylish illustrations illuminate and inform, while the easily accessible encyclopedia at the end of the book helps to explain the context and background of the stories. All combine to make this a useful and readable Bible for older children.

ISBN 978 0 85746 082 0   £12.99
Available from your local Christian bookshop or direct from BRF: please visit www.barnabasinschools.org.uk.

Enjoyed
this book?

Write a review—we'd love to hear what you think.
Email: reviews@brf.org.uk

Keep up to date—receive details of our new books as they happen.
Sign up for email news and select your interest groups at:
www.brfonline.org.uk/findoutmore/

Follow us on Twitter @brfonline

By post—to receive new title information by post (UK only), complete
the form below and post to: BRF Mailing Lists, 15 The Chambers, Vineyard,
Abingdon, Oxfordshire, OX14 3FE

Your Details
Name _____
Address_____
_____
Town/City _____ Post Code _____
Email_____

Your Interest Groups (*Please tick as appropriate)	
❏ Advent/Lent	❏ Messy Church
❏ Bible Reading & Study	❏ Pastoral
❏ Children's Books	❏ Prayer & Spirituality
❏ Discipleship	❏ Resources for Children's Church
❏ Leadership	❏ Resources for Schools

Support your local bookshop
Ask about their new title information schemes.